The Making of a Pearl

Kisha N. Davis, MD, MPH

Copyright © 2023 by Kisha N. Davis

All rights reserved. No portion of this book may be reproduced in any form without written permission from the publisher or author except as permitted by U.S. copyright law. This publication is designed to provide accurate and authoritative information in regard to the subject matter covered. While the publisher and author have used their best efforts in preparing this book, they make no representations or warranties with respect to the accuracy or completeness of the contents of this book. Neither the publisher nor the author shall be liable for any loss of profit or any other commercial damages, including but not limited to special, incidental, consequential, personal, or other damages. No part of this publication may be reproduced, distributed, or transmitted in any form or by any means, including photocopying, recording, or other electronic or mechanical methods, without the prior written permission of the publisher, except as permitted by U.S. copyright law.

For permission requests, contact EKD Mind Body:
ekdmindbody@gmail.com

Paperback ISBN: 979-8-9884577-0-1
Hardback ISBN: 979-8-9884577-1-8

Cover Design: Danijela Mijailovic
Editor: Amy Pattee Colvin

To my beloved grandparents:
Your love, guidance, and faith inspire me and leave a lasting impact
on my life and that of generations to come.

Contents

The Making of a Pearl — vii
Prologue: Grandpa Green — ix
Introduction: Humble Beginnings — xvii

Chapter 1: Foundations of Faith — 1
Chapter 2: School Years — 11
Chapter 3: Teenage Life — 21
Chapter 4: Wife to Widow — 33
Chapter 5: Life After Howard — 45
Chapter 6: Mister Gerard — 59
Chapter 7: Starting a Family Again — 67
Chapter 8: Howard's Coming of Age — 77
Chapter 9: Raising My Siblings — 87
Chapter 10: A Changing Community — 95
Chapter 11: From Peaches to Gerry — 107
Chapter 12: Our Changing Family — 117
Chapter 13: Moving Forward — 129
Chapter 14: Holy Lands, Family Lands — 137
Chapter 15: Pain and Presidents — 145

Epilogue — 154
Grandma Pearls — 155

The Making of a Pearl

When a piece of debris enters a mollusk, it does an amazing thing. The mollusk surrounds that grit with enamel to protect itself from injury. That enamel strengthens and, over the years, develops a pearl, stronger and more beautiful than the dirt from which it came.

> [12] Rejoice in hope, be patient in suffering, persevere in prayer. [13] Contribute to the needs of the saints; extend hospitality to strangers. [14] Bless those who persecute you; bless and do not curse them. [15] Rejoice with those who rejoice, weep with those who weep. [16] Live in harmony with one another; do not be haughty but associate with the lowly; do not claim to be wiser than you are. [17] Do not repay anyone evil for evil but take thought for what is noble in the sight of all. [18] If it is possible, so far as it depends on you, live peaceably with all. [19] Beloved, never avenge yourselves, but leave room for the wrath of God; for it is written, "Vengeance is mine, I will repay, says the Lord." [20] No, "if your enemies are hungry, feed them; if they are thirsty, give them something to drink; for by doing this you will heap burning coals on their heads." [21] Do not be overcome by evil, but overcome evil with good.
>
> Romans 12:12-21 (NRSV)

Prologue

Grandpa Green

Grandpa Green

Kisha and Gerard

Kisha and Gerard

The Making of a Pearl

This is a book about my grandmother. For years I've wanted to write a book about her. She's Grandma Green to me, Mother to her sons, and Miss Pearl to almost everyone else; her story is powerful.

However, when I look back on my childhood, my grandfather comes to mind first. He was tall but not imposing. He never felt unreachable, and he wasn't afraid to come down to kid level. He was silly but could quickly turn serious. I might be quietly sitting watching TV, and he would reach over and pull a pigtail, then turn quickly away so I wouldn't think it was him.

We could always depend on him for a supply of candy and snacks, his favorite being dry roasted peanuts which he chomped on despite having no bottom teeth. He always smelled a little sweet, like licorice from the Red Man tobacco he chewed. With the tobacco was the ever-present can of ejected brown spit. He would sit in his big blue recliner, watch TV and spit in the can so subtly that you almost couldn't hear the pffsst as it shot out from the corner of his mouth.

I loved sitting on his lap when he drove the tractor to cut the grass. One time he let me try to drive on my own, but I wasn't heavy enough for the tractor to register someone sitting in the seat—or maybe he just didn't turn it on all the way.

When we went out, we often went to High's for ice cream or to McDonald's for a cherry pie before heading back home, hiding the fact that we'd already eaten dessert. He loved making us Poo Poo floats, the perfect mix of ice cream and Coca-Cola.

Grandpa Green had a strategy for everything he did; maybe this came from his background as a carpenter. He tried to instill in us the smarts to think three steps ahead of whatever move we were going to make. He loved to play checkers and that triangle peg game where you try to clear the board by jumping pegs. He could do it every time, no matter where you told him to start. In checkers, sometimes I would start to make a move, and he would look at me and say, "Are you sure you want to do that?" I'd review the board and see no other move. Then three moves later, he would double-jump me and get a king. He had an eye for seeing what was hidden, like finding the four-leaf clover in a patch of shamrocks. He could always find one, and I rarely, if ever, could. He would tell me, "Just open your eyes and look; it's there."

He spoiled us, as a grandfather should. He spoiled me especially, at least according to my older cousins, Kevin and Tim. They would get me to ask him for things because he couldn't say no to Kisha. I guess I can't disagree. When I was about five years old, he got me a pony. He had built a barn for someone, and they had a pony. It was smaller than the other horses, though not one of those miniature ponies you ride at the fair. They gave it to him, or maybe he bought it. All I remember is coming home from kindergarten, and there was a horse in our front yard. It seemed huge to me, even though they said it was a runt.

We named her Dolly, and she was white with gray flakes. Now that Dolly lived with us, she needed a barn. Grandpa built one for her in our backyard at the bottom of the hill. It was a grand stable, at least to me, who had never really been around horses or barns before. For anyone with horses, it probably was pretty plain. It was two stories with a hayloft up top, which was a great place to climb up into with our friends to play.

Maybe because we were going up into the hayloft too much—or more likely, just because he wanted to—Grandpa decided I needed a playhouse. So, he built one, again in our backyard, but much closer to the house. It had one of those doors where you could open the top and keep the bottom closed, which was great for pretending to be a restaurant. And it had windows on each side so it didn't get too hot in the summer. He painted it bright pink. I dragged old rattan chairs and stools out from the house to help decorate. Those were probably supposed to be temporary, but my parents never bothered to take them back inside. Our favorite things to play were restaurant or school, but mostly my friends and I would go out there and sit and talk, or I would retreat there to read, escaping from the busyness of the house.

Our house sat at the top of a hill; at the bottom was a creek that separated us from his small one-acre farm. Grandpa had a few pigs and cows and grew some vegetables there. We kept a slop jar on our back porch for the pigs. I remember a few times, the pigs would escape from his barn and run up the hill to the back of our house. Standing on our little red back porch, when I saw them coming, I started yelling, "The pigs are coming! The pigs are coming!"

I sometimes went down with him to feed them, but he never let me get too close. I always wanted to bring a piglet into kindergarten for show-and-tell. Mom even filled out special paperwork so I could do so, but he never allowed it. I don't think he wanted me getting too close to the pigs; they were, in fact, for eating, not for playing with.

I was never really bothered when butchering day came. Grandpa and his helpers would load the pigs in his old blue Ford, take them to be killed and cleaned, and then bring them back for the butchering.

The Making of a Pearl

He had a shed behind his and Grandma's house where they would string them up. I was not permitted to go back there, but I do remember Grandma mixing sausage with the other ladies in the kitchen. I never liked the homemade sausage.

The sausage was too spicy for me and not ground as fine as Jimmy Dean. But I loved the salted ham that Grandma always pulled out at the holidays. I think you have to be raised on it to love it, and my blood pressure probably goes up with every bite. My husband, who has much more of a sweet tooth than a salty one, looks at me crazy every time I eat it. But, beyond the taste, it reminds me of family, good times, and most of all, Grandpa.

We were an animal family. Lisa, our dog, like Dolly, just appeared one day. She came before Dolly. It was when I was in pre-school, around the age of four. I had been at a playdate with a friend, we came home, and there was a puppy in our basement. Uncle Howard had gotten it for all of us, but I'll say it was for me. Maybe it was to give me something to distract me from tormenting my new little brother. Lisa was a black and brown German Shepherd mix, a mutt, really.

I liked having a dog and a pony but never really appreciated them in the way I should have. The pet I wanted and actually worked for was our cat. I had seen an article in Reader's Digest about a boy who gave up TV for a year, and his parents gave him $10,000. I had been asking for a cat for a while, and the answer was a firm no. Maybe because a new baby was on the way, and my parents didn't want the stress of a cat and a baby. Or maybe just because we were dog people, not cat people. Anyway, the story gave me an idea. I showed it to my mother and said, if I go without TV for a month, can I get a cat? I caught her at a weak moment, and she said yes, never believing that I would actually do it. Well, of course, I did.

Grandpa was always trying to trick me into watching TV. My brother Jason and I would go to our grandparent's house before and after school to catch the bus. After school, we would grab our bag of chips from the top of their refrigerator and then go into the den, or the "little room," as we all called it, to watch cartoons while Grandpa sat in his big blue chair.

Since I wasn't watching TV, I would take my snack and listen from the dining room, just out of view of the screen. One day after school, Grandpa told me to go on into the little room because he had a present for me. I walked in, and the TV was on! I ran out yelling, "Oh no, Grandpa, I can't watch TV!"

He just laughed and said, "It's okay. It's the last day of school. I won't tell if you watch."

But I didn't; I took my chips and went back to sit with Grandma, who was laughing right along with him. When I finally got my cat, I named him Reward.

Grandpa was definitely not a cat person; he said cats suck the life out of you. While we were out of town, he and Grandma would watch the house and feed the animals. He laid down on our couch for a nap and woke up to Reward leaning over his face. He about jumped out of his skin, yelling, "That cat is trying to kill me."

When Grandma later told us the story, she was laughing, saying, "Oh Gerard, he was just trying to give you a thank you kiss for taking care of him."

Grandpa was funny and loved to spin stories where you were never quite sure where the truth stopped and the tall tale started. He loved to tease us by taking his teeth out and giving us a gummy grin. I always thought it hilarious, but my cousin and little sister would run away screaming. He had a quick wit with adults, always with a side comment or joke. Rolling her eyes, Grandma would smile and say, "Oh, Gerard."

But I could see him turn serious when he needed to be. He sat up straighter, and his mouth got tighter. When he was serious, you knew it, and you didn't cross him. So, when he started telling me the story of his childhood, at first, I wasn't sure what it was. I assumed it was another tall tale or silly story.

It was a cool gray, rainy morning, and we sat in Grandma's red car in the driveway, waiting for the school bus. I was in third or fourth grade at the time. He told me he was about my age when he stopped going to school and that I already had more education than he ever had. I was waiting for the joke to come, but his posture was serious, not playful, and the joke never came.

He went on to tell me that he was the youngest of four. He shared that his mother died in childbirth, having his next sibling who also didn't survive. His father remarried but later died when he fell off a roof. His stepmother put him out to work on a farm when he was about ten.

At that moment, the school bus pulled up. I bounced out of the car, said, "Bye, Grandpa," and bounded onto the bus, glad to be free of the tense conversation. I remember him looking somber but not quite sad; definitely no tears. I had never heard any of this story before, and I wasn't exactly sure what to do with it. It weighed heavy on me then, and I carry it with me to this day.

How different our childhoods were. Mine, so worry-free; his so traumatic. And yet it never stopped him from becoming a great man. He never got into trouble with the law. He focused on providing for his family and doing well by the community. He took the scraps he was given, turned them into something special, and helped others do the same. Construction was his love language. He built barns and playhouses for me, but for the community, he built houses. He loved giving people a start so they could make a living for their families. His greatest wish was for his children and grandchildren to have the opportunity to choose their own destinies rather than have someone else choose them.

That afternoon after school, when I got off the bus, seemed like any other afternoon. We ate snacks and watched TV. He smiled and joked and made no mention of that morning's conversation about his childhood. He never mentioned it to me again; he didn't have to. The message stuck.

Introduction
Humble Beginnings

Humble Beginnings

Gary Green

Lethia Matilda Mason Green

The Making of a Pearl

But be doers of the word, and not merely hearers who deceive themselves.

James 1:22 (NRSV)

To understand my grandmother, you have to understand where she came from. She has a spirit of perseverance that is in her DNA and was brought up with a faith that has carried her through many trials and tribulations.

Ida Pearl Hallman was born June 18, 1918, in the small farming town of Quince Orchard, Maryland. How fitting that pearls are the birthstone for the month of June. Quince Orchard was a small farming community about twenty miles northwest of Washington, DC. Her father, Samuel Hallman, was originally from Martinsburg, Maryland. Her mother, Evelyn (Ricks) Hallman, was born and raised in Quince Orchard. The homeplace where my grandmother grew up was right next to her grandparents. Between the two properties were twelve acres owned by the family. It wasn't much, but it was significant for a Black family to own land.

The original land patent for Quench Orchard dates to the 1760s and was given to Henry Claggett. Somewhere along the line, the name was changed from Quench to Quince, and as far as we can tell, this area was never the home of any quince orchards. The area was composed of Whites—some slave owners, some not—and Blacks, some enslaved and some free. In the early 1800s, a man of Irish descent by the name of Nathaniel Mason came to the village of Dawsonville, Maryland, and met Lucinda Simms. They were blessed with eight children: Isaac, Rosetta, James Edward, Henry, Lloyd, Lucinda, Mary, and Lethia Matilda.

Many of the Mason children remained in the Dawsonville vicinity as they grew into adulthood; however, Lethia Matilda Mason did not. She ventured to the village of Darnestown in her daily routine, where she met a talented enterprising carpenter and builder named Gary Green. They married, acquired property, and built a homestead. They were blessed with twelve children: eight sons, Alexander, Alonzo, Ernest, Eugene, John Wesley, Robert, William Edward, Vernon, and four daughters, Emma, Ida, Jimmy, and Jane.

The children were born several years before, during, and following the Civil War. Union soldiers camped nearby, and local women and children were cautioned to be wary of the foraging men in blue.

Humble Beginnings

Maryland was a border state and officially a Union state but was right next door to the Confederate state of Virginia. Maryland was also a slave-holding state and home to many Confederate sympathizers. Until slavery was officially abolished in the nation, there was always the threat that a free Black could be kidnapped and sold South into slavery. It was an uncertain and desperate time at best, especially for a young family with infants and small children on the edge of the confederacy.

I heard this story many times growing up, at family reunions and celebrations of a family historic site. And while it makes mention of the existence of slavery, it refers to it as something distant, far away, that did not touch us. It gives the impression that this family could be White—a man of Irish descent—though, of course, we knew ourselves to be Black. But if Black, certainly free.

Free to marry, venture out and acquire property. However, as my brother began to dig deeper into our family history, it confirmed everything we knew but added another dimension we did not. None of the elders in my family ever talked about the presence of slavery in our family, and even when directly asked, they said it did not exist in this area. That changed when we found their names on an 1864 slave census.

Gary Green was enslaved by John Higgins in Rockville. John Higgins owned one other slave, Mary Coates. John Higgins later became mayor of Rockville and had a long family legacy of founding the city. In fact, both Gary Green and Mary Coates are named in a book written about Higgins and the history of Rockville.

Gary's wife, Matilda, was owned by Sam Higgins and worked on his farm. It is unknown what type of work she did or how extensive the farm was. This area of Maryland did not have large plantations of cotton or tobacco that happened further south. Most of the farms in this area were subsistence farms with fruit, veggies, cows, pigs, and chickens that mainly fed the family that lived there, and excess would be sold. Gary and Matilda were enslaved by cousins John and Samuel Higgins, who lived ten miles apart. Their twelve children, eight boys and four girls, remained on the farm with their mother.

It was crucially important for Maryland to remain part of the Union and prevent Washington, DC, from being surrounded by Confederate territory. President Abraham Lincoln delivered the Emancipation Proclamation on September 22, 1862. It declared all slaves in Confederate states to be free as of January 1, 1863. It did not, however, apply to slave-holding northern states such as Maryland. Maryland freed its slaves, effective November 1, 1864.

The Maryland legislature approved compensating slave owners for the financial loss of their slaves. In 1867, the state began collecting names of enslaved persons as of 1864. As this was tied to financial compensation, keeping a detailed record was in the owners' best interests. It turns out former slave owners were never given money for their losses, and the real benefit of those records comes to us, the descendants, to know just a piece more of our history.

This fact brings more questions than answers. If Matilda Mason was a slave, then we can likely assume that her father, Nathaniel Mason, was too. He is listed as a man of Irish descent; was he a slave? Was he the product of a White slave master and slave or of a consensual relationship? How did he make his way to Dawsonville— of his own free will, or was he sold there? In the first two decades after the Revolutionary War, several slaveholders freed their slaves.

In addition, numerous free families of color had started during the colonial era with mixed-race children born free as a result of unions between White women and African-descended men. Although the colonial and state legislatures passed restrictions against manumissions and free people of color, at the time of the Civil War, slightly more than 49 percent of the Blacks, including people of color, in Maryland were free, and the slave total steadily declined after 1810. By this time, about half of the Blacks in Maryland were free, even more so in Montgomery County as opposed to the eastern shore where there were more plantations and famous former slaves such as Frederick Douglas and Harriett Tubman once lived.

We are told that Matilda Mason "ventured to Darnestown in her daily routine." Was that of her own free will in support of her family, as required by her masters, or was she sold? How did Gary and Matilda meet and raise a family while living ten miles apart? All questions without answers. The only answers live in my DNA.

In 1864 life changed for Gary and Matilda; they gained their freedom. While their opportunities were now greatly expanded, their physical location did not change much. An 1870 census shows them living, now together, on the same street as Matilda's former owners. Their family expanded to now include a total of twelve children, one of them being Vernon Green, my grandfather's father. Another was Emma Green, my grandmother's grandmother.

Gary Green and the other men of the area saw a need for education. Gary Green, along with James Ricks and Carlton Mason, formed an association to provide a school for the children of the

Quince Orchard/Darnestown area. They acquired a one-acre lot on September 18, 1868, to be held in trust "for the purpose of erecting or allowing to be erected thereon a schoolhouse for the use, benefit, and education of the colored people of Montgomery forever" per Montgomery County land records.

The association and their neighbors constructed a schoolhouse on the property and independently hired a teacher. In March 1874, Gary Green appeared before the Montgomery County Board of Commissioners to request funds for the payment of the teacher at Quince Orchard Colored School. The Board agreed to pay, provided the lot and schoolhouse were conveyed to the County Board of Commissioners.

On April 14, 1874, Gary Green, James Ricks, and Carlton Mason conveyed the house and lot to the county commissioners for the sum of $5.00 to be used "exclusively for the education of colored youth of the neighborhood."

The Ricks, Masons, Greens, their neighbors, and their descendants were educated at the Quince Orchard Colored School. As they grew into adulthood, three Green sisters, Jimmy, Jane, and Emma, married three local Ricks boys, Ernest, Washington, and John. The marriage of Ernest Ricks and Emma Green produced ten children, the third of whom was Evelyn Ricks, born in 1898. Evelyn went on to marry Samuel Hallman. Samuel was born in 1889 in Martinsburg, Maryland.

They were married at Emory Grove Parsonage on February 23, 1916. They both worked on the Hegdon Farm in Quince Orchard, Maryland, and lived there until two weeks before my grandmother's birth on June 18, 1918. Samuel was supposed to go into the service for World War I in June, but he got a reprieve because his child was due to be born. The war ended later that year, and he never had to enter the service. Samuel and Evelyn bought a house from John Ricks at a cost of $1,200. After moving into their new home on Riffleford Road, Evelyn became strictly a mother and housekeeper while Samuel continued to work on the farm. They had eight children, of which Pearl is the oldest.

It is from this stock that Pearl got her start. Her great-grandfather and his friends, newly freed from the bonds of slavery, had the foresight to purchase land from their former slave owners. While they physically built a church and a schoolhouse, what they also created was a grounding and centering for the Black community in Quince Orchard. It created the foundation that would produce teachers, lawyers, doctors, and dentists. But most importantly, it created a sense of belonging, community, and connectedness in a community that was just beginning to thrive.

Gary Green went on to be a delegate to the Republican National Convention. This Quince Orchard community also had one of the first Black postmasters, John Ricks, in 1899. Pearl's family remained in the Quince Orchard area from the 1860s and the end of the Civil War through the present. I today remain in this community on land that was once my grandfather's farm.

Grandma's early years were hard but mostly happy. They were poor but didn't know it and had everything they needed on a little twelve-acre farm.

In the following chapters, the layers of my grandmother's faith unfold. Grandma attributes that faith to the Bible stories her mother told her during her childhood. However, I would argue she learned it not just from the Bible stories her mother told, but it was evidenced daily in the community where she was raised.

Her great-grandfather, Gary Green, and his friends stepped out on faith. When the world around them was telling them that they shouldn't succeed, they did. They steeped the community in education and church in ways that bleed through even to my generation. When Grandma hears Bible stories, she can see and bear witness to similar experiences in her own family and community.

Chapter 1
Foundations of Faith

Foundations of Faith

50th Anniversary of Evelyn and Samuel Hallman, Pearl's parents

Back: Henry Jackson, Howard Bell, Esther Lyons, Upton Hallman, Helen Thompson, Pearl Green, Eugene Hallman, Thompkins Hallman, Gerard Green, Sr., Sylvia Hallman, Roberta Hallman, Gerard Green, Jr., Melvin Hallman

Middle Row: Darlene Jackson, Pamela Jackson, Vernon Green

Front Row: Evelyn Ricks Hallman, Samuel Hallman

The Making of a Pearl

Now faith is the assurance of things hoped for, the conviction of things not seen.

Hebrews 11:1 (NIV)

Author's Note: *In the story that follows, you will read my grandmother's story in her voice as it unfolds from her perspective, followed by my reflections on her life.*

When I was four years old, my grandmother—my father's mother—Emma Hallman, passed. The only thing I can remember was cousin Alexander Green had an old Ford Model T. It had two little round windows in the back, and you fastened leather windows on the side to close it when it was wintertime. He took Papa, Mama, and me to the funeral in Martinsburg, Maryland. The hearse was drawn by two beautiful black horses with two men sitting up front. This was the first time I had ever seen a car, let alone get to ride in one. There was a large crowd of people who attended, and I remember thinking she must have been an important woman. I didn't really know many of the people because we rarely visited Papa's family.

I grew up on a farm, and that meant work, but it also meant fun. I had a wonderful time swinging on the old swing. Papa made it from an old rope he found in the barn and made the seat from a board off the fence. Papa would push me, and I laughed with glee. It was spring, and the daffodils and irises were blooming. The sky was a beautiful blue, and the clouds, here and there, were as white as snow. From out of the house came the smell of hot rolls and fresh pies. Mama loved to cook and bake.

In the cool of the morning and evening, Papa would plow the garden and show me how to plant the seed. Potatoes always had to be planted by St. Patrick's Day, and other vegetables later. I loved following my dad around and watching the birth of piglets and calves. What an exciting time. When my brothers were born, I had to share Papa with them. I did not mind; he had enough love for all of us. He showed us how to milk cows and feed the chickens, ducks, pigs, horses, cats, and dogs.

One event we always looked forward to was Camp Meeting when Mama would fix dinner of fried chicken, fresh string beans, rolls, pies, cakes, and all the other goodies. We would ride in the old horse and buggy to the campground and meet all our aunts, uncles, and grandparents. We could play for a while, but then church started on the campground, and we had to go sit and listen.

In the summer, Mama had us wash jars for her to put vegetables and fruit in for winter. We had all kinds of fruit trees: apples, plums, peaches, pears, and cherries. Mama climbed the trees with us to show us how it should be done, telling us to pick the bucket full before we ate some, which was very hard to do.

I remember when Papa used to shuck corn in the fall, and the weather would be so cold. Mama would bundle me up in coats and scarves, and I would run out to where he was. He would take a few of the discarded corn stalks and wrap me inside them so I could stay warm while he cut another set of corn. I can only imagine what I must have looked like, a little bundle covered in a brown mound of husks and stalks.

I had Mama and Papa all to myself for the first four years, then my brothers and sisters started coming. It seemed like every other year another baby was coming. My brother Sam was born on March 15th, 1922. I don't remember much about him being a baby, but he was mischievous as a child. He was named after my father. On January 2, 1924, Thompkins William, a second son, was born. He was named after my mother's two brothers—Thompkins and William Ricks.

For a little extra money, Mama provided boarding for the schoolteachers that taught at Quince Orchard colored school. Mr. Dye was the first teacher to stay with us, and I started elementary school under him in 1924. One morning, Mama sent me upstairs to knock on Mr. Dye's door because he was late for breakfast. She told me to knock on the door and wait for an answer; she specifically told me not to go into his room. I didn't listen.

I entered his room and called his name and again heard no answer. I went back downstairs to tell Mama, who then went back up the stairs to discover he had died in his sleep. I was too little to even think that I should be scared. I don't know why he died, a heart attack or stroke maybe. We had so little interaction with doctors that we often didn't know someone was sick until they were on their deathbed. I didn't know then how close to doctors and my own sick bed I was about to become.

Later that same year, I started having trouble with my foot. I was six years old, and I came home from school with a wound on my foot. It had been there for several days, and I wasn't too worried about it. But one day, it really started hurting. I showed it to Mama because it

The Making of a Pearl

hurt so much. Especially as we walked the two miles back and forth to school every day. When she first looked at it, I saw worry in her eyes, but only for a second. She sent me upstairs and later came to put a salve on it and told me to rest.

I didn't go to school the next day, and the doctor came to look at it. Both events were strange. Mama always sent us to school, even when we had a cold. I was sleeping, and when I woke that morning, the sun was up, and I wondered why Papa hadn't called me to get the eggs and help with the cows. I started getting dressed when I heard Sam crying. As I was headed down the stairs, Mama told me to go back up and rest and that I didn't have to help Papa with the chores that day. I was so happy to hear that. But I could hear my friends out the window asking if I would be walking with them to school. Mama said, "No, not today."

Mama brought me breakfast in my room, something she had never done before—such a special treat. Later Dr. Upton Nurse came to look at my foot. He said not to worry and that I would be okay. But then, I overheard him whispering to Mama and Papa. He told them they needed to take me to the hospital so they could do some more treatments on my foot. I wasn't sure if I should be scared because Dr. Nurse said not to worry.

I was right to sense something was wrong, even as I enjoyed the special treatment. That was the beginning of many hospital stays, one of which nearly cost me my foot.

Dr. Nurse sent me to Children's Hospital in Washington, DC, where I stayed for a long time. At the time, I had long red hair, and my Godmother and namesake, Pearl Ricks, would come to the hospital twice a week to comb my hair. Despite this, the nurse decided to cut it all off, saying it was too difficult to manage.

After being in the hospital for a long time, the doctors decided they needed to amputate my leg at the knee to save my life. Mama and Papa came in on Sunday to sign for them to go ahead with the operation. I was so scared and worried and started praying for a miracle to save my leg.

While I was in the hospital, I was allowed to go to the playroom. The director, Mrs. Wells, was deaf and wore a hearing aid around her neck for us to talk through. She had heard that they were discussing taking off my leg, so she decided we should have a talk. She said to me, "We must believe that God will take care of us. If you do have to lose your leg, God gave you two hands and a gift to use them. With your willpower and faith, you can make it. Whenever you feel down, think of the gift of your hands."

Then she taught me how to crochet and make flowers out of crepe paper. These creative tasks came naturally to me because of my gift from God. Those gifts have always been a comfort to me and a way to make extra money. When I was home from the hospital, I would make all kinds of paper flowers. I would sell them for $1.00 a dozen.

Every church in the area had bouquets of flowers that I had made. And I was proud to be able to help provide for my family. Crocheting continues to be a comfort to me even today. I mostly made afghan blankets, but also some clothes. Now I like to crochet slippers that we give to those staying at nursing homes and homeless shelters. I also crochet prayer shawls to give people a little warmth and comfort when they are going through an illness or difficult time.

On the Monday after my parents signed the papers, a new nurse came to work at Children's Hospital. After looking at my foot, she begged the doctors to let her take care of it for two weeks before deciding to take it off. They agreed. This nurse told me that she had another very similar case where she was from. She put a red liquid on it that looked like Mercurochrome, but she called it something different. My foot improved so much under her care that doctors did not have to remove my leg. She was an angel of mercy. I went back and forth to Children's Hospital several times during my childhood, but never again did they talk about removing my foot.

When I left the hospital for good, the nurse told me always to take care of my foot myself and I would be fine. To this day, I still do. I watch it, bathe it, and take special care of it to prevent getting wounds. I have had lots of problems with my foot since childhood, and many times when doctors threatened to cut it off. But by faith, I have always come through. It may have slowed me down, but it has never stopped me.

Despite my youth, the events around my foot were when I learned to pray, to believe, and to have faith that God was always with me. Before going to the hospital, my parents always took us to church. My mother was a Sunday school teacher. Every night and every Sunday morning, we had to gather together to say prayers. On Sunday evenings after church and dinner, we would all gather around Mama, who would sit in an old rocking chair in the living room and read us Bible stories. Each story had questions and answers after it, and Mama made sure we learned the stories well.

The Making of a Pearl

On July 11, 1927, my brother Upton Montgomery was born. He was named after Dr. Upton Nurse, our family doctor. I remember Upton having two teeth when he was just two months old. After one of my trips to the hospital, I came home to find Mama pacing with Upton. She had not visited me in the hospital this time, but that was not unusual. It was harder for her to get away to visit me with all of the little boys, so I didn't think anything of it. Upton had a very bad case of whooping cough, and I could hear my mother praying to God that she would not lose him. I think that is when I learned how strong her faith was and how important it was to pray.

I remember coming home from the hospital another time on crutches, and that Sunday was children's day at church. Mama insisted that I take part, so I stood up in front of the church on crutches and sang, "O Come All Ye Faithful." My parents never pampered me because I was crippled. I thought they were being mean to me.

Sometimes having a lame foot made me feel I couldn't do as much around the farm, but my parents never lowered their expectations. One day I asked Mama, "Does Papa really love me?"

She looked at me, hugged me, and said, "Your Papa loves you with all his heart, and I do too. You were the firstborn, and you are a girl, and he feels that you are extra special. It may seem like we don't love you, but we want you to be strong in the soul and be able to take care of yourself and not let being crippled be an excuse for not doing your best."

I don't think I appreciated it then but thank God I had parents that taught me how to do things myself.

Reflections on Foundations of Faith

Grandma tells this story of her childhood matter-of-factly. They were going to cut her foot off, then an angel came, and they didn't. She usually clucks and laughs when she gets to that part and says, "It was a miracle," and then moves on to other happenings. After several more weeks of hard work, she was discharged home, never to return to Children's Hospital again. However, her foot—and the trials and tribulations because of it—continued to be an issue throughout the rest of her life.

We never really knew what caused the problem. As an adult, a doctor once asked her if she ever had polio, and she replied that no one ever told her that. He said "interesting" and nothing more, leaving her always to wonder if he suspected she had polio. None of the typical characteristics of polio fit her situation. She didn't have other polio symptoms, such as fever, sore throat, and stomach aches. Neither did she have paralysis that traveled through her body. Nor was polio typically treated with amputation, so the suggested course of treatment to cut her leg off would also not likely apply to polio.

Most likely, she developed a wound that progressed to an infection in the foot, possibly due to the rubbing and irritation from her shoes on her heel, which she often complained about on her walks to school. That infection likely progressed quickly and deeply, possibly to the bone. Such an infection could easily be treated now with a course of antibiotics before spreading. However, penicillin was not discovered until 1928, and the general public did not commonly use antibiotics until the 1940s.

Also, recall her brother Upton suffering from whooping cough, known these days as pertussis, as a baby.

These diseases, that we rarely think about today, could be devastating back then. Polio would ravage communities, leaving children that survived paralyzed in its wake. Parents lived in fear that their children would become stricken. Pertussis infected hundreds of thousands of children, and thousands died each year before a vaccine was developed. The polio vaccine, first developed in the 1950s, was a turning point.

We take many of these medical advances for granted today. Unfortunately, these days antibiotics are often used in excess, resulting in antibiotic resistance and the risk of rendering their curative effectiveness useless.

Distrust and fear have led many to forego vaccines. We all benefit from the low prevalence of many preventable diseases due to the widespread herd immunity that exists because of vaccines. Recent measles outbreaks in communities with low vaccination rates evidence just how important vaccines are, but they offer the biggest benefit when everyone gets them. The COVID-19 epidemic has brought to light for everyone how fearful and disrupting it can be to live in a world without adequate treatment or vaccination for an illness.

Over her life, Grandma lived through multiple surgeries, debilitating arthritis, and more threats of amputation. It is interesting to imagine how her life would have been different had the leg been removed when she was six. Would she have been treated

The Making of a Pearl

like she was disabled and had limitations placed on her abilities? Would she have been as likely to marry and have children and work? How would being confined to crutches or a wheelchair have limited her ability to travel the world? Would her years of pain, hospital visits, and biweekly trips to the podiatrist have been reduced?

It was not uncommon to see a man with a leg amputation, usually related to his participation in the Civil War or World War I. Though many surgeons had honed their techniques out of wartime necessity, it was then, and is still today, rare to perform this procedure in children. A Danish study of childhood amputees from 1899-1964 showed the children fare quite well as adults, most of them advancing in education beyond that of their childhood caretakers, and they had equal rates of marriage and childbearing as the general population. However, that study was done in Denmark and did not have the degree of racial segregation that we experience in the United States.

A poor, rural Negro girl in the 1920s has few things going for her in terms of her likelihood of advancement. It is doubtful that she would have had the same access to prosthetics and physical therapy that would have been afforded White children of the time. Much of her life is made up of walking—walking a mile to and from school each day; walking five miles to catch the bus to Washington, DC for work; walking door-to-door to sell Fashion Frock dresses or Avon; walking the Holy Lands. Those experiences are much less likely as an amputee. Her world likely would have been smaller, her opportunities more limited. Others have depended on Pearl throughout her life. I wonder how her life would have been different if she needed to depend on others more.

Just as fire strengthens ore, her faith has been tested and honed because of that foot. Through every infection, surgery, and setback, she learned to call on God. Grandma prays with a faith that comes with the assurance that what is needed is already taken care of. It will work out because God has already worked it out. When asked where that deep faith comes from, she says from her mother's knee. When asked where my faith comes from, I say it is from my grandmother's foot.

Chapter 2
School Years

School Years

Quince Orchard Colored School

The Making of a Pearl

Keep hold of instruction; do not let go; guard her, for she is your life.

Proverbs 4:14 (NRSV)

Mama and Papa bought their house on Riffle Ford Road in Quince Orchard, Maryland, just a few weeks before I was born, and it seemed like they built just enough house for the family they had, not the family they would have. Sure, it started with just me, but I ended up being the oldest of eight.

First, it was Sam, then Thompkins, then Upton, then Gene, then Melvin, then Roberta, and finally another girl—twenty-one years after I first took my first breath in 1918, my final sibling was born, another girl, Esther.

We lived in a two-bedroom old country farmhouse on a few acres of land where my father kept me busy tending to all the farm responsibilities—feeding the chickens and milking the cows. I tried to avoid feeding the hogs whenever I could. It wasn't because they were dirty, but one of my uncles once told me that a hog would eat anything—even a little girl. He was a bit of a jokester, so he may have just been kidding, but I wasn't taking any chances.

Our little farm wasn't much, but at the exact same time, it was. It was significant for a Black family to own land, and we lived next door to my mother's parents. Between the two properties, the family owned twelve acres. We used to go over to Ma and Pa's house—that's my mother's mother and father—after church to have picnics and dinner, and then the whole family would gather there once a year for the family reunion.

You'd have to be careful not to step in a mud pie—what we called cow dung—but if you kept your head on a swivel, you could have a pretty good time. Beautiful trees bore every type of fruit. They were perfect for climbing and made for exciting games of hide and seek. But I found myself most excited when I got to sit on the porch with my grandmother and hear what it was like growing up in Quince Orchard during her day.

Honestly, the town hadn't changed all that much. The one-room schoolhouse we walked to every day at one point held 121 pupils was the same white, wooden structure my mother and grandmother had attended. The land that the schoolhouse sat on was purchased in

1868 by some men in the community, one of them being my great-grandfather, Gary Green.

It always seemed so profound to me that a few Black men, a few short years after the end of the civil war, would put their own livelihood and safety on the line to purchase land and build a schoolhouse. But as my mother would say, "They looked around the community and saw a need. They were doers and doers do."

I don't know if she made that up herself or stole it from the back of a TIME magazine, but either way, that story still serves as a guiding light for my life. Doers do.

By the time I started going to the Quince Orchard Colored School myself in 1924, it was no longer the same building that my grandmother had inhabited for her learning. No, unfortunately, that building burned to the ground in 1901. There were whispers of arson, but nothing was ever proven. Some believed that one of the teachers was an activist, and the segregationist forces in Quince Orchard wanted to send a message to him and, consequently, to all of us. But we persisted.

We ended up getting a new school, but here's the craziest thing—the county school board promised a new school to the community when the old school burned down. But guess what they did. When it came time to build a new school, they felt more comfortable building a new school for the White students than the Black students.

They ended up moving that old schoolhouse for the White children across the street and putting it on that three-acre piece of land that had been purchased in 1868. I think the point was that we weren't good enough for the new school. Instead of giving something new to the colored students, they would give something new to the White students, and we would get the White students leftovers. Thank goodness our community still owned the land!

We got our workbooks the same way. It was rare to get new books. Instead, we would get the leftover books that White students had already used. Often pages were torn out. Words like NIGGER shouted from the margins, suggesting that "An ignorant person was here." That was always hard. We learned to ignore the words screaming at us in the margins, but it was hard to fully understand a topic when you only had half the lesson.

We had to work twice as hard to learn the same material. But I always loved hearing the story about the schoolhouse being the same schoolhouse that the White students used. There were no walls ripped out. Although they tried to make me feel less by not giving us

The Making of a Pearl

the new school, they made me feel equal by proving that we were just as good as the White students and could use the exact same school that they had used the day before.

My parents constantly told us that we were just as good as anyone else, and here was proof—here it was in black and white or brick and mortar that we were equal. Now don't get me wrong, compared to all the amenities that my great-grandchildren have now, it would appear that we were all equally disadvantaged back when I was going to school.

There was no school bus to pick us up on the street corner. We walked. We walked on sunny days. We walked on rainy days. We walked in the snow. If there was school, we went. People had bled, sweat, and died to give us the opportunity to be educated, and we weren't going to miss it. Besides, if you stayed at home, you had to work. Papa always had another job for us to do, and I was happy to get off the farm.

Of all the kids that attended the school, our house was right in the middle. In the mornings, I would peer out the window and wait until the Ridgley boys made their way down from Darnestown. I'd join the pack of students headed toward the school, and we would pick up more children as we went like a snowball rolling down a hill. Mrs. Sadie Green was always taking in boarders—orphans sent to Quince Orchard from Washington, DC. I don't know if she got any money for it or if she just liked the company, but almost every semester, there was a new name to learn.

One foster boy, Bernard, never really liked going to school and always fell behind the rest of us in walking. We moved at a reasonable pace because the last kids to get to school had to clean the room, and I had no interest in doing that. The bigger kids would put the smaller kids on their shoulders to make better time. Well, one day, Bernard was lagging behind as usual until we crossed by Mr. Jones' farm. That day Mr. Jones had left his dog unchained.

We navigated the farm without any incident; perhaps there is strength in numbers. But Bernard was dilly-dallying behind by himself. Turns out Bernard was pretty quick when he needed to be. He ran right past us with that dog nipping on his heels all the way to the front door of the schoolhouse. Willie Ridgley fell on the ground laughing so hard we were late. But cleaning erasers was a small price to pay for that sight. Blazing Bernie kept that nickname for decades.

Small wooden desks took up most of the room in the building, accompanied by a series of standard chairs that you had to slide into

School Years

from the side because the desktop was attached. The cool kids had scratched their names or initials into the desks, but if you were smart, you only did that when it was time for graduating because if you got caught, the punishment was much worse than writing on the chalkboard. Writing on the chalkboard happened to be my punishment for talking. And I loved to talk. Miss Clarke would make me write on the board a hundred times. I will not talk in class. Though we both knew it was going to happen again. And soon.

Some years there weren't enough desks for all the students, and the women in the community would throw a dinner trying to raise money for desks and supplies. Seven grades were all taught in that same one-room building. The classes would be grouped together—the first graders were all the way to the left, and the seventh graders were all the way to the right. One teacher taught all those students, and if you listened closely, you could learn the lesson for the grade above you. The older students would help the younger students with their assignments, allowing the teacher to move from grade to grade.

A camaraderie existed between the grades and the students that I'm not sure you get today. Part of that was, frankly, because schools were segregated. Because of segregation, all the Black kids were bussed to one school. That said, it was hard for my parents to explain why we could play with White kids in the neighborhood, but when it came time for school, we went to separate schools. The fact that all of us Black kids were at the same school allowed us to get to know one another very well. And the teachers were of the community. They loved and cared about us, understood our feelings, and inspired us to achieve.

My favorite subject was always arithmetic. I loved figures until we got to geometry. That was a struggle. Even now, with figures, while other people use calculators, I'm using my pencil. They say the pencil is so slow. I would always keep the machine there with me. If I felt like I was wrong, I'd use the machine. Most times, I was right.

Sometimes when walking to school, which meant walking over a mile from Riffleford Road to Quince Orchard Colored School, my foot would swell. Sometimes when I was preparing to leave school, my teacher would ask the high school bus driver if I could ride the bus back to Riffleford Road. On those days, when I got home, I had to bathe that foot in hot water.

When I was in elementary school, the boys and girls would play around together coming up the road from school, but the boys never bothered me. They stayed their distance as if I had the plague. This made me sad and led me to feel that no one outside of my family cared about me.

Winters when I was a child were very cold, and it snowed from November until spring. Mama insisted that I wear long underwear, but the children at school always teased me. So, I would pull them above my knees so you couldn't see them below my skirt. Then on the way home, I would stop at the mailbox and pull them back down before going up into the house.

With three brothers around, Sam, Thompkins, and Upton, I treasured having some girly things to play with. I had a beautiful doll that my Godmother, Aunt Pearl, gave to me. Each year for Christmas, I would get a new outfit for her. Just after Halloween in 1930, I found a beautiful baby layette set my mother was making. It was hidden under the bed. I was so excited because I knew this would be for my doll. I was right to be excited—but for the wrong reasons. Just a few weeks later, my brother Eugene arrived, and I learned who the layette set was really for.

When I was a little girl, I wanted to be a missionary. I could picture myself going out in the world singing. I would sing and teach; that was my goal. Singing to people, teaching people. And I've done that all my life. When I was a little girl and had trouble with my foot, I knew then that I wouldn't be able to travel overseas. Mama used to sing "The Peace" to me to help comfort me.

> "If you cannot cross the ocean,
> and the hither lands explore,
> you can find the heathens around you,
> you can find them at your door."

And she said, "If you cannot preach like Peter; if you cannot pray like Paul, you can tell the love of Jesus, you can see them at your door." She never gave me an excuse not to serve others.

I finally finished primary school after being out sick so much. I had kept up with my schoolwork and skipped some grades, which helped me stay in classes with my friends.

Reflections on School Years

Public schools for Whites or Blacks were still rare in the South in the 1800s. Black slaves were forbidden from receiving a formal education. While the majority of the planter class hired private tutors to educate their children, no system existed to educate poor Whites. Churches provided a rudimentary education to the poor.

In the early 1860s, the Freedmen's Bureau began establishing schools in the south, and by 1865 had opened over 1000 schools for Blacks across the country. Reconstruction was the first entry of taxpayer-funded formal public education for both Blacks and Whites, though most jurisdictions created and maintained segregated schools.

Segregation in schools would be cemented by the 1896 Supreme Court decision in Plessy v. Ferguson, which codified the separate but equal framework that would persist for decades to come. In this period after the Civil War, schools for colored children started popping up all over the country. Teachers were paid from government funds, and there was a rise in teachers, both Black and White, male and female.

The Quince Orchard Colored School was founded during an explosion of support for the education of Black youth. However, that initial enthusiasm waned as conservative Whites regained control in the post-reconstruction era. By the early 1900s, the country continued to see an expansion of public schools with more taxpayer support. More districts were offering high school, and education was beginning to be seen as a way of advancement.

However, the attitude toward the education of colored children was also shifting. Across the country, there was a sharp decrease in funding allocated to Black schools and increased violence toward them. In 1901 the Quince Orchard Colored School was burned, and though no one was ever charged or even accused, many suspect it was due to arson. It was a perceived attempt to send a message to the school's activist teacher and the community that promoted Black advancement.

While the county school board initially promised to build a new school for Black students, instead, a new school was built for the White students, and their old school was dragged across the street. County support for the school was lacking, and while the school board did continue to financially support the teacher, upkeep for the school fell mainly to the community. Additional support was also given to the teachers through room and board. Families like my grandmother's housed the teachers and provided their meals. This provided extra support for the family and helped to recruit the teacher into the community.

The Making of a Pearl

Grandma's school experience was typical of most rural children, Black or White, in that area. Small one-room schools that taught all grades together fostered a sense of community; kids knew one another across grade levels. For her, the ability to hear what the grades above and below her were learning allowed her to make up for missed school due to her foot without falling too far behind. However, just having a school in the community is not always enough to overcome the challenges of being able to attend.

My grandfather, several years before, also attended the same one-room schoolhouse. However, his family did not or could not place the same emphasis on education as Grandma's. He and his brothers weren't allowed to start school until late November after the harvest was finished. He spent the winter months trying to catch up, often spending lunch with the teacher to learn what he missed, only to have to leave school again in the spring to help get seeds in the ground.

Even the little bit of schooling he did receive ended at the age of nine after his father died. At that point, his stepmother removed him from school and forced him to work as a laborer on a nearby farm. He grew up quickly, essentially a man from that point on. He would spend the week on the farm and return to his homeplace on the weekends.

He returned one weekend to find that his stepmother had sold off most of the furniture and all of the livestock except a few chickens that must have outrun her. But at least she didn't sell the house, and it remained with him. He did all he could to keep the house going. Initially, with the help of his brothers, but they soon moved away. He maintained it on his own throughout the rest of his teen years. He later moved his first wife, Emma, and stepdaughter Helen in with him.

For Grandpa Green, education beyond the basics was a luxury not afforded to him. And in that small rural town, examples of folks using education to change their station in life were few and far between.

Chapter 3
Teenage Life

Teenage Life

Ida Pearl Green

The Making of a Pearl

Train up a child in the way he should go; and when he is old, he will not depart from it.

Proverbs 22:6 (KJV)

Mama was always selling things to help make extra money. She would sell beautifully decorated chamber pots. I always thought it was so funny that we would have such ornate pots to do our business in. We would hitch up the horse and buggy and go visit the White families on our street. Everyone knew Mama, and the ladies would open the door for her. She would never start by saying she was there to sell something; she would ask how they were doing and visit with them for a while.

If they told her they had company coming, she would say that she had just the thing that would make them feel welcome—a new chamber pot! Or if they were feeling down, a new chamber pot was just the thing to brighten their day. Mama always knew just what to say. She began to be known for how good a saleswoman she was. Later when she was working at the Breylove farm, the ladies would have her take their goods to the market to sell because she was more successful than they were.

Because Mama sold chamber pots, we always had beautiful pots in our house. But it didn't make what was inside them any more beautiful. No one knew that better than our teacher Miss Johnson.

We were all expected to empty our chamber pots each day. For us kids, as soon as you could carry your own pot, you had to start emptying it. This also went for the teachers that boarded with us. Mama provided a room and meals for the teachers, but emptying their pot was their own responsibility.

Miss Johnson was running late one morning and rushing to dump her pot. She was already dressed for school, and us kids saw her rushing out of the house and across the yard to the outhouse with her pot in her hand. Thompkins said, "Why is she dumping her pot with her nice clothes on? She might get something on herself." Well, not even a minute after he said that she tripped and spilled the entire contents of the pot on her dress.

Her eyes welled up with tears, and between sobs, she yelled out, "Who uses these stupid pots anyway." Thompkins, Sam, and I were cracking up laughing. I even saw Mama briefly crack a smile before she put her serious face on and told us kids to be respectful. She

Teenage Life

rushed out to help Miss Johnson back into the house and get cleaned up. We tried hard not to snicker as they walked by us, but one of us, probably Sam, let out a chuckle. Mama gave him a severe look, and he got quite a beating later. She always taught us not to make fun of another person's hardship.

It was important for Mama to know she was bringing us up the right way. She was loving, kind, and a great cook, but she was also a stern disciplinarian. She truly believed that if you spared the rod, you spoiled the child. Mama was quick with a switch or whatever she had handy to beat you with if you acted up. And she always did it right when you acted up. She never said she was going to do it later. And there were never any second chances.

Mama's younger sister had come to live with us. She teased me something awful. She always knew just the right buttons to push to get me to say the wrong thing, then she would run and tell Mama, and I would get in trouble. One time when I was about fifteen and she was twenty, she did something, and I called her a name. We were in the house, and then she ran right outside to Mama, who was hanging the clothes on the line to dry. I can still imagine seeing her through the window, talking to Mama, and pointing inside at me.

As she speaks, I see Mama's face harden, she stops hanging the clothes, and I see her marching towards the house. She grabs a switch on the way. I knew I was about to get it. I didn't wait a moment longer and ran right upstairs into my room, shut the door, and crawled under my bed. I knew I would be safe there. I could hear Mama coming up the stairs, boom, boom, boom.

The door flew open and yelled at me to come out from under the bed. I knew better than to do that, so I just stayed there, hoping that if I didn't make a noise, she wouldn't know I was there and would leave. I was wrong. Next thing I knew, off came the mattress, and off came the box spring, and Mama was beating me through the bed frame. I looked up in terror and caught the rage in her face with her arm raised, ready to hit me again. Then she seemed to freeze. She stopped. Her arm was in mid-swing, then she dropped the switch, turned around, and walked out. That was the last beating I ever got.

Papa, on the other hand, was much quieter, and he usually left the disciplining to Mama. We never saw them fight or disagree. Sometimes we would ask Mama for something, and she would say no. Of course, we didn't like that answer, so we went out to ask Papa. Whenever we asked him something, he would always just turn back to us and ask, "What did Mama say?" We would just sulk back inside

The Making of a Pearl

because we already knew what Mama had said. He never did overrule what she said if we didn't like her answer. Papa was most concerned with work, getting everything done when it was supposed to be done.

I had a good childhood filled with love but also with pain. My brother Samuel was very jolly as a child and always into something devilish. In the spring of 1934, around his twelfth birthday, he got sick. We thought it was from eating too many early apples, but after a few days, he did not get better. Mama took him to Dr. Nurse, who gave him medication and told us to bring him back if he didn't get better in a few days. Later he told my father to go to Washington, DC, and get some serum because Samuel had acute meningitis and that this was his only chance of survival.

The doctor told us that this medicine had a 50 percent chance of saving and a 50 percent chance of killing him. Samuel did not survive. What a blow to our close-knit family. We were all devastated, but Mama comforted us by saying, "He has gone away to be with the Lord, but we will see him again."

In those days, the death of a sibling was hard but not uncommon. Most of my friends' families had lost someone along the way. We came to see death as a part of life. We missed our loved ones but trusted that they were with God and in a better place.

During my first year of high school, Papa was out of work. Mr. Hedgon had sold his farm. Papa began working down in southern Maryland, putting in a new road. By this time, Mama had one miscarriage and two more sons—Eugene, who I named after a friend of mine, and Melvin. To keep the family going, Mama went to work at Albert's, a farm across the field from us.

Papa went down to his sister Eleanor's and brought back her daughter Sophia to help take care of the kids so I could attend high school. Sophia only stayed with us from September to December. After she went home for Christmas, she never returned. Mama still had to work at the farm during the day, and we would clean the house with her after she got off from the farm in the evening.

By February, Papa decided he was not keeping the kids anymore. So, I had to stop my first year in high school to keep house. In frustration, I promised myself I would never return to school again. I had struggled so hard to get to high school, and then this happened. I was already behind my friends because I had to stay back in elementary school because I was so sick. I was embarrassed to be so far behind my friends and figured it just wasn't meant for me to finish school.

Teenage Life

On the first day of September 1934, Evelyn Roberta, my first sister, was born. She was named Evelyn, after my mother, and Roberta, after my mother's midwife, but we called her Bertie. All I could think about was Mama having another baby for me to care for. This meant I would be washing diapers for Melvin and Bertie. So, while Mama was home for a while with Bertie, I found myself standing and waiting for the school bus so I could go back to school. I got over my earlier frustration, but I still felt very sad because the friends I had made the year before were now a year ahead of me. But school seemed better than taking care of two babies. I made up my mind that I was going to finish high school.

Melvin used to throw tantrums when he didn't get what he wanted. One time he wanted something—he always wanted something—and Gene wouldn't give it to him and then started teasing him. Melvin fell out in a tantrum, crying and flinging himself to the ground. Mama was inside and saw and heard it all from the window. She came out and grabbed a switch of the pear tree. She picked him up by one arm and started beating him, saying, "Melvin, this is enough of this! Don't you let me see you out here throwing yourself on the ground again!"

Melvin and Bertie seemed to get into everything. They were always playing around; they especially liked to sit and get warm by the potbelly stove when it was cold outside. All the boys wore long johns with the flap in the back to use the bathroom. One time Melvin got too close to the stove, and the flap caught on fire and burned his back. I can still hear his screaming as we all rushed to throw water on him to put the fire out. His clothes were stuck to his back, and his skin was gnarled and red. I could see the worry in my parents' faces, even though they didn't speak of it.

They took Melvin to see Dr. Nurse, who dressed the wound. They had to take him back and forth to Dr. Nurse several times a week for many weeks until his backside finally healed. Dr. Nurse said, "Well, now that it's healed, you can give him a proper spanking for getting too close to the stove."

Mama responded, "No, I think with all of these dressing changes, he's had more than enough punishment for one little boy."

From then on, Melvin always sat up very straight and proper. After he died, the undertaker said he still had a small area of his back that was scarred from where he had been burned.

Most of our activities in high school centered around the church. Our youth group got together on Sunday afternoons for Bible study.

The Making of a Pearl

If we were lucky, there would be a movie at church or a softball game, but mostly we would just hang out. None of us had a car, and where would we drive to anyway? We didn't have money to go out to eat, and no restaurants were nearby.

Sometimes there would be dances, and I would go to watch my friends, but I was never much for dancing. It seemed like I could never get my feet to work how they were supposed to. I can't blame my troublesome foot; I was just clumsy. Mostly we would hang around Snyder's Store or sit in front of the telephone pole, talking and laughing. We all had more than enough work to do on each of our farms to keep us busy and out of trouble.

The girls stayed mostly separate from the boys. Though some of my girlfriends were starting to partner up with boys, it never seemed like any of the boys wanted anything to do with me. We didn't talk at all about where babies came from. Girls were told to keep their skirts down and boys to keep their pants up. You weren't allowed to be alone with a boy. For the longest time, I thought babies came from kissing. I didn't have any older siblings or even cousins to tell me the way. It wasn't taught in school, and it certainly did not come from my parents. I guess somehow, along the way, I just figured out the birds and bees from whispers and gossip.

Just because the boys weren't attracted to me doesn't mean I didn't try to attract them. The children always had Sunday school before church, and I would take myself and my siblings to class. One day after walking them to school, I went next door to my cousin Emma's house. She and I pinned up our hair, put on make-up, and got fancy for church. We got there just in time for church to start. We looked so pretty.

My parents said nothing about it, but that doesn't mean it went unnoticed. The sermon that morning was about disobedience. The pastor looked at me and said, "When your mother sends you to church early for Sunday school, and you go next door and paint your face, that's disobedience." At that point, I didn't want to be pretty anymore; I wanted to be invisible and disappear into my pew.

Christmas was the time when family and friends would visit throughout the neighborhood. It was also a time to see who was visiting who and how long they stayed. Mama made so many delicious cakes, pies, and punch to have ready for any guests that would come by. I remember one neighbor, Isaac. He had two sons, one tall and thin, the other short and fat and slow of mind. Isaac would always come over for Christmas and bring Mama a little embroidered handkerchief as a gift. It wasn't much, but Mama would always fuss over it like it was the greatest thing in the world.

One Christmas, I could see from the window that many people, some of them my friends, were over at another house. I heard them laughing and singing as they walked down the street and continued right on by our house without stopping. Disappointed to be passed over, I asked Mama, "When am I going to have company?"

Mama said, "I'll let you know when you can have company." Isaac and his sons happened to be there and overheard the whole situation. Isaac's slow son laughed "Kee ke ke ke." I wondered what was so funny, and it just made it hurt more like he was laughing at me for not having friends. Even in a house filled with people, I could still sometimes feel lonely.

When I finished high school, I was so proud. I didn't think graduation day would ever come for me. I had so many starts and stops because of my foot and helping to take care of my brothers and sisters; that day was a big day. In our senior year, all the girls took sewing, and in class, we made our dresses for class night and graduation. Our dresses for class night had to be pink or blue. Mine was blue and white for graduation. We had a prom. For that, Uncle Johnny's girlfriend dressed me up in one of her fancy dresses and helped do my hair and makeup. I felt so pretty.

The prom was held at the school; they had dressed the building up really nice. I didn't have a date. We all went as one big group. We graduated from Rockville High School. My parents came and all my siblings. Papa asked me if I wanted to go to college. With all the stops and starts in my schooling, I couldn't see myself going to college. I told him no; my ambition was to make sure all my brothers and sister made it through high school and maybe college. I did whatever I could to help support them in their schooling and was proud to see each of them walk across the stage with their high school and even college diplomas.

Reflections on Teenage Life

It is striking how severely and swiftly Pearl's mother doles out discipline. With each subsequent generation, it seems to have mellowed. My father tells of some epic spankings he received, but they don't measure up to my grandmother's stories. Of the few spankings I had, I distinctly remember them hurting my father more than they hurt me. And my oldest son still laughs at me for hurting my own hand when attempting to give him a spanking. The threat of spankings was usually the most that I levied, which was usually enough to correct behavior.

The American Academy of Pediatrics and most other medical societies now discourage spanking, noting the emotional damage it can cause, including increased anxiety, depression, and aggression. However, in general society, views on spanking still remain largely in favor, with more than 70 percent of Americans saying it is sometimes appropriate to spank a child.

As I've grown as a parent, I rarely turn to spanking, partly due to the warnings from the AAP but mostly because I never found it to be that effective. In my own growing up, the guilt of disappointing my parents has stuck with me far more than any spanking ever did. And with my own children, I have other tools in my parenting toolbox to mold and guide them. I'm proud of the young men they are becoming without me resorting to physical punishment. Aggressive beatings as a form of punishment to force one into obedience is a vestige of slavery that I am happy to let pass by.

School for Grandma was interrupted due to illness related to her foot. But also, because she needed to help meet the needs of the family and care for her younger siblings. During the Great Depression of the 1930s, her father lost his job, and her mother had to go back to work to help support the family. While this small farming community, in many ways, was insulated from the depression because they made their own food and clothes, the economic downturn did still reach and affect them in meaningful ways.

One man she knew of lost all his money when the Poolesville bank collapsed. After that, he never trusted banks again, and he kept all his money in a can in the outhouse. One day he was burning brush, and the outhouse caught on fire. Everything burned, his money included. Bank or no bank, he was never meant to get rich.

Everyone of that generation knew a story of someone losing everything. My grandfather never trusted banks and often kept money hidden in safes in the house. We are still waiting to find some big stash of cash that he had hidden away. It's been over thirty years since he passed, so if it exists, we are not likely to find it.

While Grandma's father's job loss forced her mother back to work and kept Grandma home to run the house, it also solidified her commitment to finish school. That commitment to education came in handy years later as she eeked out her own existence.

Teenage Life

Many coming-of-age details are missing from the story of her teen years. Puberty and menstruation were not discussed, nor how babies were made. Pearl's mother's pregnancies were always a secret to her until the baby arrived. It would be naïve to assume that just because people didn't talk about sex, that it didn't happen.

That lack of sex education most certainly did result in pregnancies. However, those surprise pregnancies often resulted in shot-gun weddings and whispered pregnancy math when it was discovered that the wedding date and likely conception date were too close together. It was rare to see a single mother, and when you did, most often, she, not the father, bore the brunt of the community's disdain.

My grandmother's lack of sex education at home stands in stark contrast to my own upbringing. Possibly my father rebelled against those conversations that he never had. Or possibly his time as a school counselor, where he saw way too many teen moms, prompted him to share freely with my siblings and me about the birds and the bees. Those conversations started with him reading the book "Where Did I Come From" to us in elementary school. The education continued as he peppered us with car conversations on smart choices in middle school.

It culminated—for me at least—while I was in college with a most humiliating condom on a banana demonstration when my then-boyfriend, now husband, and I were getting ready to embark on a weekend jaunt to the beach. While my mother seemed to prefer that we think sex never happens, my father's message focused on being with someone worthy of that gift of self and keeping your own future and wishes in mind.

Grandma, like most teenage girls then and now, longed to be with her friends. And she, too, carried many of the same doubts that teenage girls carry today—am I pretty; will boys ever be attracted to me? The story of her rolling up her long underwear or sneaking to her cousin's house for makeup reminds me of my own attempts to change into more provocative clothes when my parents were out of sight.

During Pearl's youth, birth and death come up as part of everyday life with little of the fanfare or excitement we place on them today. The births of her siblings as well as the death of Sam and the miscarriage of another baby, are treated with equivalent matter-of-factness. In Pearl's day, women didn't have elaborate baby showers or fancy maternity wardrobes. Nor did they spend a

The Making of a Pearl

lifetime mourning a child that was lost. Children were born or buried without much commotion. Excitement or grief was quickly incorporated into the daily rhythm of life without time for emotion.

Chapter 4
Wife to Widow

Howard and Pearl Bell

The Making of a Pearl

Yea, though I walk through the valley of the shadow of death, I will fear no evil: for thou art with me; thy rod and thy staff they comfort me.

Psalm 23:4 (KJV)

Starting from when I was a girl, I had dreams that would come true, though not always in the way you would want them to. One time I had a dream about my friend Sarah; she was getting married. It took place in church, and she wore a beautiful white gown with gorgeous flowers. The church was packed with people. I remember waking and thinking it strange that I couldn't see the groom's face. I ran downstairs, excited to tell my mom about the beautiful dream.

Before I could get very far, she told me that she just learned that Sarah had died. A few days later, we went to the funeral. So much of my dream was the same as what I saw in the church that day. The flowers were the same, the people were the same, and even the dress she wore in the casket was the same wedding dress she wore in my dream. It dawned on me then that the groom I couldn't see was death. I didn't realize then what a large role this gift would play in my life.

Education was important to my mother; she wanted all of us to do something beyond high school. College was not in the cards for most Black kids from Quince Orchard, though my younger siblings would prove that to be wrong. From the time I was in the hospital with my foot and Miss Wells taught me how to do things with my hands, I became good at music. I used to make flowers and play the piano at church. I completed a music correspondence course through the US School of Music.

After I finished high school, I met Howard Bell. He lived in Sugarland, just under ten miles away. We started courting in the spring and would meet up on Sunday evenings after church with the other young people. I considered myself grown, but Papa still had me cutting and sawing wood to help the family. One day I was out working in the yard and saw Howard coming down Route 28. I ran into the house because I didn't want him to see me working in the yard. A few weeks later, he revealed that he was in on my secret, saying, "I saw you out there cutting wood. You don't have to hide yourself from me."

The first time he took me up to Sugarland to visit his family, I was excited but also nervous about what I should say or do. When we drove up to his house, I saw his younger sisters, Charlotte and Edna, in the yard picking up wood chips. I got out of the car and jumped right in to join them. I was used to doing that at home and wanted to be helpful. Howard gave me the strangest look and asked, "What are you doing?"

"I'm trying to be helpful."

He replied, "Come on in this house, you are here with me, not here to clean the yard."

I was embarrassed but also grateful that he didn't expect me to clean his parents' house.

One day Howard decided to take me to Rockville to go to the movies. I had never been to a real movie theater before. Sometimes they would show a movie at the church or school, but that wasn't the same as a real theater. I was excited to sit in the seats and watch a real movie on a big screen. When I told my parents where we were going, Mama asked, "Why do you want to go to Rockville to see a movie? The church will show it in a few months."

"Mama," I said, "I don't want to just watch a movie at the church. I want to sit in a real theater and see a movie on the big screen."

"Pearl, be careful. Stay close to Howard. Rockville is not Quince Orchard," she cautioned. "And don't wear your good church shoes."

I ignored her. Of course, I got dressed up and wore my best shoes. I was so excited to go to a real theater and see a real movie. The movie projector at the church always seemed to break down halfway through, and someone would have to fix it. The little kids were always making noise, and Mama usually sent me to take care of them.

Howard and I got to the ticket counter and bought our tickets, but then the clerk told us to go around back. Howard said, "Why should we go around back? The entrance is right here."

The clerk said nothing but pointed to a sign—"Colored entrance in the rear." So we went around to the back, where there were stairs to walk up to the balcony. The seats down below looked so comfortable with soft red cushions, but our seats were wooden and hard. The floor was sticky, and I don't think it had been cleaned for weeks. Right away, I wished I had taken Mama's advice. They crammed us in tight. Every seat was taken. But down below, there was lots of room. It didn't make sense to me why they would have us all crammed up there when there was so much beautiful, comfortable space downstairs.

This was my first experience with segregation. It wasn't my first encounter with White people. We interacted with them quite

The Making of a Pearl

regularly. My parents worked on a farm, and their bosses were a White couple. We always called them Mister and Missus; I assumed this was because they were the boss, not because they were White. We played with their kids growing up, and Mama even had them come to the house. There was even a group of White ladies that lived on our street. They would get scared during thunderstorms and come up to our house to wait the storm out. But we never went to school with those White kids. It was just the way it was, and at the time, I didn't think anything strange about it.

After the movie theater incident, I started noticing signs of segregation all around me. We didn't have it so much in Quince Orchard, but once I left our community, it felt like it was everywhere. We didn't have any restaurants in Quince Orchard, but if we went to eat in the city, we would have to go around back to order. A White man, one of Papa's bosses, used to come to our house and ask for him. Mama would answer the door and say, "Good morning, sir."

He'd reply, "Send Sam out." She would invite him into the house, but he would never come in; he'd just stand on the porch outside and wait.

I would see this and say to her, "Mama, he is so mean. Why doesn't he say hello or good morning or anything? He just asks for Papa, doesn't even say please or thank you."

"He probably was never taught to say that. Pearl, you should be nice to everybody regardless of how they are. And you should always say hello and good morning, good afternoon, or good evening to everyone you meet."

At the time, I never thought he acted this way because he was White and we were Black, but now I know that was why.

Howard and I were married in December of 1938. When we were first married, we lived with Howard's Aunt Charlotte in Washington, DC. Howard drove us everywhere, and he thought it was important for me to learn to drive too. So he taught me. It was difficult at first, but eventually, I learned how to work the clutch.

I enjoyed driving and liked to be able to take myself where I needed to go. For so long, I'd depended on Papa or Howard or the bus or someone else to get me where I needed to go. Howard even took me to get my license. I was so scared during the driving test but so excited when I passed. I really felt like an adult.

One day Howard told me he had gotten a ticket and needed to go to the courthouse to pay for it. He had me drive him there, so of course, I stayed to listen. He also had several of his friends meet us there. It seemed strange to me that he was making such a big deal of this ticket. Well, come to find out, he hadn't just gotten a ticket for speeding; he had gotten a ticket because he didn't have a driver's license.

I was shocked. How could he not have a license when he was the one who taught me how to drive? I shouldn't have been surprised. Back then, it was rare for Black folks to get or even need a license. When we were in our community, it was rare for the police to come and disrupt it. Eventually, Howard did get his license, and I drove him there to get it.

The funny thing about being the oldest of eight is that you don't know you will be the oldest of eight, but the kids just keep coming. I could never tell when Mama was pregnant. With her being pregnant so many times, you would think I would have learned the signs. She was a big woman, always wearing an apron, so you could never really see her belly. The following June, Howard and I were still living with his aunt in Washington, DC, when I got a call from Mama asking me to come home and help wait on her because my sister Esther had just been born.

I couldn't believe it, another baby. And here I was, twenty-one years old, grown and newly married, and my mother still didn't tell me she was expecting a baby. So, I moved back home, helped her, and helped take care of my other brothers and sisters. That is just what you do when family calls; you help.

After I finished helping Mama for a few weeks, I moved back to DC with Howard. I started doing day work—cooking and cleaning—to help us have some extra money.

We moved into a new house in August of 1939 in Lincoln Park, the Black section of Rockville. We didn't have any furniture. We fashioned pillows out of feed bags, and eventually, we got some old furniture from my parents. We were just so happy to have a place of our own and get into the rhythm of our life.

Lincoln Park was about ten miles from my parent's home back in Quince Orchard. But it might as well have been next door as often as I went back to visit. We were there most Sundays for church. I still played the piano for the service and taught Sunday school. On the Sundays we didn't go back home, we would go to a large African American congregation in the center of town. When we did go home on Sundays, we often stayed and had dinner with my family. We would go back to our house loaded up with leftovers to help get through the week.

The Making of a Pearl

We would sometimes get together with our friends Gerard and his wife, Emma, and my cousin Emma and her husband, Ellsworth. We would go together to baseball games on Saturday nights and other events at the church. Church was really the only place that there was to go.

Gerard had a stepdaughter named Helen. Helen's parents never married, and Gerard married her mother, Emma Baker, when Helen was five. Gerard's wife, Emma, died in 1942 at the age of thirty-two when Helen was just fifteen. We told him that he would have to take care of Helen now. He was the only father she'd known.

It was hard back then to be a single mother. And even harder to find a husband willing to be kind to your child. But Gerard didn't mind that Emma had a child. He raised Helen like his own daughter. He would braid her hair and make sure she looked nice. He said he learned to braid from braiding pigtails on the farm. After Emma died, Gerard and Helen had some hard days, but they always maintained a strong bond.

Not long after Emma died, Gerard was drafted for World War II. He was worried for Helen and wanted her to be well taken care of. Gerard arranged for family friends, the Branisons, to take care of Helen. He dropped her off and then took his papers to report for duty. The first few days were filled with paperwork and medical examinations.

Surprisingly he didn't pass the medical examination. They told him he had asthma, so they could not use him. I never knew him to have trouble breathing before or after that, but he sure was thankful to have asthma that day. He came back home, picked up Helen from the Branisons, and went right back to raising her. She went on to get married in 1945 and have five children of her own. We always teased her that she was making up for being an only child. Gerard built a house for her and her husband, Charles Thompson.

In the summer of 1940, I was excited to learn that I was expecting. I was due in February of 1941.

One early morning in October 1940, I woke up from a dream. I was thankful it was just a dream but fearful that perhaps it was more. My sudden rise also woke Howard, who had been gently snoring beside me. He asked me what had startled me so significantly. As a tear trickled down my cheek, I told him it was nothing.

He said, "Now Pearl, you know your dreams come true. So tell me, what did you see?"

I told him. "We were driving in the car going down Route 355—the main road from Washington, DC, to Frederick—and someone turned in front of our car. That caused an accident, and you were killed."

He consoled me and said, "Okay, okay, don't you think anything more about it. Everything is going to be alright."

The next day, Howard went to get his haircut in Seneca, a Black town. And he put on his favorite suit. He was so handsome. He spent the rest of Saturday and Sunday going up to Seneca, Quince Orchard, and Sugarland and saw all his family and friends, and had a great day of church and fellowship. When we got back to the house, he held me all night. And that was the last time he held me.

I had gotten a new job so that I would have a little bit more spending money. Howard was carrying me to Rockville to my new job. That Monday, on the way home, we were traveling down Route 355 when a car made an illegal turn in front of us, and as Howard swerved to miss the car, he lost control. I was thrown from the car and couldn't really move. He was trapped inside the car.

He talked to me until the paramedics arrived, and I was taken away. I heard one of the medics say that Howard was dead. I didn't understand it because I was just talking to him. Apparently, it took his last bit of strength and focus to comfort me. They took me to a doctor's office, but because of Jim Crow, they took me down to the basement. I sat alone on a cold, hard chair and waited for the doctor to come. I was about six months pregnant at the time. The doctor pushed, knocked, and punched around my stomach and finally said, I'm not quite sure to who, "She's alright. The baby's alive."

The policeman said he would take me home when he had finished his run. They put me in a chair at the courthouse to wait. When his shift was over, he came to carry me home. He asked me if he should take me to our house in Lincoln Park, and I said no because there was no one there. I had him take me to my parent's house. I sat in the car while he rapped on the door and asked if they knew anyone named Ida Pearl Bell.

Papa came and carried me into the house. And then he went off to figure out what had happened. I went up to my old room and went to sleep. I don't remember that evening or even the next morning. My room wasn't mine anymore, I had been gone for twenty months, and Esther and Bertie had taken it over. Mama must have told them to sleep somewhere else, or I just slept hard in my grief because I don't remember anyone coming in.

The Making of a Pearl

They took me to Dr. Nurse the next day. He said, "Well, you're looking fine, but I need to give you the facts. You can worry and grieve for your husband and bring a deformed baby into the world. Or you can put it behind you, move on and bring a healthy baby into the world. The choice is yours."

From that day, I never cried or screamed or anything. It was a dream. It never happened. I just shut it out of my mind completely.

Dr. Nurse was the first person who looked me in the eye and talked to me directly. Of the medics at the scene, the doctor who checked the baby, the policeman who brought me home, no one directly told me Howard was dead; I just overheard it. No one expressed compassion or even pity for me. I felt like a rag doll just being pushed around and passed along. During that time, I couldn't really feel anything. I felt invisible, like no one could bring themselves to talk to me.

They wouldn't let me go to the funeral, but I did visit Howard at the undertaker's shop. I put my hand on him until it was cold up to my shoulder. Stone. And I knew that he was gone. On the day of the funeral, I watched the funeral procession carry him up the road. I sat at that window and had no tears. I don't know how I did it. I had a choice, and I decided to live for my child. No crying. No sadness. I picked myself up and kept going.

Reflections on Wife to Widow

Howard introduced Grandma to many things—movie theaters, driving, and a world outside of Quince Orchard. Her time with Howard was the first time segregation and Jim Crow rules were thrown in her face. It was her coming of age both as a woman and new wife, as well as living in a segregated society. Before that, in the comfort and isolation of Quince Orchard, she was insulated from the humiliation of being treated like a second-class citizen. But she couldn't stay in that bubble forever.

Grandma's premonition powers are legendary in our family. She has an uncanny way of knowing what would happen. At one point, my mom was intentionally collecting Grandma's stories, and one day Grandma said to her, "I dreamed you were writing a book about me."

I first directly encountered the story of her dreams when I was in high school. I would stop at her house on the way to school each morning for breakfast. She'd often serve me blueberry muffins or waffles with fried egg whites and sausage. I inherited my distaste for egg yolks from her. She would pray and read from the Upper Room daily devotional magazine. We would swap stories about my life and hers. Those breakfasts are where I heard many of the tales that form the bones of this book.

One morning I was excited to share with her a crazy dream I had the night before. Something about Jesse Jackson and hot air balloons. She stopped me before I got very far and said, "My mother always told me not to tell your dreams before breakfast because they might come true." She went on to tell me her dream about Sarah and the groom that ended up being death. She then shared the dream of Howard's death. I had heard of this whispered family lore from my parents, but it was my first time hearing it from her for myself.

She told the story with the same matter-of-factness that Grandpa had told me about his parents a little more than six years earlier. No tears or sadness, no signs of regret or reminiscence on what was lost or what could have been if she hadn't shared her dream before breakfast. I was thrust into the day's routine carrying this piece of her story. I headed off to school with similar mixed emotions that I held years before. Some relief to get away from the heaviness of it all. Some pride in feeling that I could be trusted with the story.

Much in the way that a mollusk walls its irritant off from itself by forming a shell of nacre around it, Grandma walled off a piece of her hurt. For her, that was necessary to be able to keep going. So many women, especially Black women, spend their lives burying pieces of themselves to protect themselves from their hurt. The love of a strong family and the support of her community helped polish Grandma so she could shine like the Pearl she is rather than becoming sullen and bitter or dull and lackluster.

As a family physician myself, Grandma's relationship with their family doctor, Dr. Nurse, is significant to me. He returns to Grandma, yet again, at the beginning of what will be a difficult road ahead. He gives her the respect of talking directly to her and shares what she needs to know, even if she doesn't want to hear it. I am a staunch proponent of having a primary care physician—someone who knows your life story and will give you the whole truth about your health.

As a physician, I can't imagine telling my patient to bury their grief and just get on with their life. The death of a spouse is traumatic, especially for someone so young and pregnant. While his words seem cold, I understand Dr. Nurse's desire to be frank with

Grandma in the context of the world that she lived in. He knew that wallowing in her grief or sinking into a depression would not bode well for her or her baby's future.

In fact, several studies have shown the negative effects of depression on pregnancy. Depression during pregnancy increases the overall risk of adverse birth outcomes, including pre-term birth and low birth weight. Recent studies show this risk to be even more elevated in African Americans. During Grandma's time, there were no medications to treat depression; it was faith, family, and getting back into a routine that guided her through. Dr. Nurse surely knew that she would be wrapped in the loving arms of a family and community that would support her.

Chapter 5
Life After Howard

Little Howard and Mother Pearl

The Making of a Pearl

> *Be strong and courageous. Do not be afraid or terrified because of them, for the Lord your God goes with you; he will never leave you nor forsake you.*
>
> *Deuteronomy 31:6 (NIV)*

After Howard died, I moved back home with my parents. I never went back to the house that we had built. My son arrived in February of 1941. I had him at home with a midwife. I named him Melvin Howard after my brother Melvin and his father, Howard. But we always just called him Howard.

Now it was Mama's turn to wait on me and my baby. Once Howard was a few months old, Mama said, "A house shouldn't have too many adults." So, she and Papa went to live with the Breyloves, where they were working. I helped care for my younger siblings, including my new sister Esther and my son Howard. They were just a year and a half apart.

My parents would come home every evening to make sure I had everything together for my siblings—their lunches packed, their clothes washed and ready, and their studies done. The older boys would help with the things on the farm, like feeding the hogs and milking the cows. At least I didn't have to do that anymore. But there was no shortage of things to do on the farm. Mama and Papa would always come home on the weekends, and we would all go to church together on Sundays. They made sure that I had everyone up and ready for church. I wasn't upset about having to do the work. It was good to be around family during this time.

It was hard being a single mother, but I was blessed to have the support of my family. Everyone in our small little community knew what had happened, so no one looked down on me or thought I had done something wrong to be a single mother. Howard fell right into line with the rest of my brothers and sisters. As he got older, he would help Papa in the fields and with other farm chores just like everyone else.

Mama wanted all of us to continue our schooling after we finished high school. I got married not long after graduating, so I hadn't gone to school. But Mama encouraged me to go back to school. So, I started a correspondence school with the US School of Music based in New York. I always enjoyed music and started playing the piano for the services at Pleasant View. I graduated from the program in 1942. It was a good way to fill my time while the older children were at school.

For the longest time, I couldn't understand how it was that Howard had died. I had been thrown from the car in the accident, and the baby and I were both okay. He was still talking to me after the accident, so how was it that he died?

I got my answer again in a dream. He came to me one night and opened his shirt. He showed me how the steering wheel had pushed against his chest, breaking his ribs and puncturing his lungs. I then felt like I could understand what had happened. But it also changed me. I stopped dreaming. Anytime I felt myself starting to have a dream, I would wake up. Some nights it felt like I got no sleep at all. I also learned that I couldn't dwell in the past and on bad things that had happened; I had to move forward. Little Howard needed that.

Life was hard for me after Howard died, and I was grateful that I could live with my parents. Eventually, I started doing day work again. My first job was as a domestic, cleaning houses and cooking for people, mostly White folks. I had always helped my mother with cooking and cleaning, but it was a new experience doing it in other people's houses and by their rules.

It surprised me how stingy people could be. I remember one woman I worked for; she always had lots of extra food for her guests but never shared any of the leftovers with the other staff or me. I got smart. When I cooked the pork chops, I would cut off a little piece of each one. Once the big ones cooked, you couldn't tell a piece had been removed, and I got a decent dinner.

I started working for a lady who lived up the road. I cleaned the house, scrubbed her floors, and washed her diapers. And I got a dollar a day for my work. While I had done lots of cooking, cleaning, and washing at home, doing it for someone else helped me realize that it was not something I wanted to do for a living. I started to look at other things I could do for work. At that time, we were starting to see advertisements to do government service.

You had to take a test. How you did on the test would determine what types of jobs you were qualified to do. I wanted to qualify to do secretarial work, anything that would take me away from cleaning and washing. I took the test and felt like I had done well on it. I was proud of how my teachers had prepared me for it. But, at the same time, I knew it was a long shot. While more and more of the men from our neighborhood were entering government service or the military, there weren't many women who got to do so.

The Making of a Pearl

At the time, I was working for the Eisenhower family—no relation to the President. I had been with them a while when they moved into one of those houses on Quince Orchard Road going to Gaithersburg. Mrs. Eisenhower had just had a new baby, so they moved to the new house to have more space. The new baby brought lots of new work, and to get there, I had to walk quite a bit further than where they had been before.

One morning while I was walking to their house for work, I decided I was going to ask for a raise. After all, I was cleaning their whole house, doing all the washing for the baby—so many diapers!—all for just one dollar, and now I had to walk extra far to get to them. As I was walking, I practiced what I would say to Mr. Eisenhower in my head. I figured I would start out by being nice and reminding them how good a job I was doing and how much they needed me. Then when they agreed, I would ask for the raise. How could they turn it down?

When I got to the house, I was ready. I said, "Good morning Mr. Eisenhower."

He barely looked in my direction and said, "Um hmm. The chamber pots are in the room, ready to be emptied."

"Mr. Eisenhower, can I talk to you? I was just wondering, since Missus had the new baby, who is just a bundle of joy, there is a lot more washing and cleaning to do. And this new house you have is a lot bigger than the one you had before. And since you have moved, I must walk a lot farther to get here than I did before. And Missus has said that she really thinks that I am doing a good job. So, I was just wondering if I could have a raise. Maybe twenty-five cents more for all the extra work that I am doing. I'm happy to do it, but I have a family to support, and the more work and the longer walk takes me away from my son for a lot of time during the day."

Mr. Eisenhower turned and looked at me for real, this time with burning fury in his eyes. He stood up, his anger growing every second. He said, "How dare you ask me for more money. You are just a poor farm girl. If it wasn't for us, you wouldn't have a job at all and would just be picking up wood chips or feeding slop to the pigs. What does a girl like you need with a dollar and a quarter a day? In the good old days, we wouldn't have had to pay you at all. It is not my fault that you have a baby out of wedlock like all these other women running around here with their pickaninny children. Maybe you should have thought about having mouths to feed before you went and laid up with some nigger. You should be grateful for people like us who are willing to give you such generous pay already. Now, go into the house, wash all these diapers, and then walk back home at the end of the day."

I felt so defeated. I wanted to cry and scream, but I knew I couldn't give him the satisfaction. Big Howard's death taught me how to hold in my emotions. So, I stiffened my lip, set my face, and said, "Yes, sir. Thank you, sir." I turned and went into the house.

I set about washing and cleaning. There probably were a few tears mixed in with the wash water that day. I worked, and I prayed all day, "Lord, please help improve my lot." As I walked home in the evening, I thought, *How could I be so stupid to have asked him for more money? Maybe I should have asked Mrs. Eisenhower, or maybe I should have written it in a letter. How could I get across to them that I was worth more?*

As I was walking home, I always stopped by the mailbox to get the mail. We didn't get much mail, and I rarely got any. Maybe a letter from Aunt Pearl now and then. I got lots of letters after Howard died, but I never read any of those. It was kind of a big deal when we did get mail, so I was surprised to see a letter in the box. I reached in and pulled it out. It looked very official and was addressed to me. I stood right there at the box and opened it.

It was a letter saying, please report for government service. The very next day, I called the government service and went on down there and got everything situated. They had a job for me at Bituminous Coal.

The next week I called Mr. Eisenhower. "Hi, Mr. Eisenhower. This is Pearl."

"Pearl, where are you? You didn't come back. We have been expecting you."

"No, Mr. Eisenhower, I won't be back. I'm working for the government service now."

"You're in the government service? I don't believe it; you are too stupid to do a job like that. What is our government coming to if they will hire someone like you?"

"Well, if you want to come up here, I'll show you the papers because I will not be back!"

It didn't even matter what he said to me anymore. I always knew I was worth a lot more than what he said. My family, my church, and my community taught me that I had value. And now the government was confirming it with a job and more money than I had ever had.

The Making of a Pearl

Mr. Eisenhower taught me how to stand up for myself and to know my own value.

I had my first real job with the Bituminous Coal Division (BCD) of the Department of the Interior. The office was all the way down in Washington, DC. After Howard died, I also stopped driving. I had never driven much, but after the accident, I didn't trust myself to be behind the wheel. This meant I had to walk everywhere or depend on others for my transportation.

Papa always saw that we got to work. He would always carry us to our jobs or wherever else we needed to go, but we always had to pay him for gas. Every day on the way home, he would stop and get fifty cents worth of gas. After getting the government job, Papa would take me to catch the 6:30 am bus in Rockville to take me downtown Washington, DC. This was around 1943, and Papa had started working on a farm in Rockville.

Sometimes I would stay with him on the farm at night so we wouldn't have as far to go in the morning. We had a car—if you could call it that. It only worked about half the time. My father would go out at about five o'clock in the morning, get his breakfast, and try out the car. And if the car didn't start, he'd wake me up, and we'd walk to Rockville to be there when that bus came up. It always seemed so cold on those early morning walks, even in the summer.

I would lead the way, with Papa walking behind. He always said he was protecting me from anything that might come up. The thing I did need protection from were the dogs that we would pass at the fork in the road with two big beautiful farmhouses on either side. Two big black dogs would see us coming and start barking.

They would run along the fence beside us and keep barking until we were out of view. We walked a little faster for that stretch of the road. We would then continue down the lane and on to Rockville. Papa never let his children have an excuse not to go to work, and he instilled in us the value of hard work.

Workdays were long, and it felt like I barely got to see little Howard at all. He was still asleep when I left, so that only left the evenings for us to spend time together. I am so thankful that I had my family to take care of him while I was at work. Upton was the main one to watch over him, in addition to my mother, of course.

He had chores to do just like we all did, getting eggs from the hens, helping clean the barn, and weeding the garden. He would sit with Papa when he drove the tractor to plow the fields, and when he was older, he learned to drive the tractor himself. Many days I would come home from work and find him sitting outside eating an ear of corn that he had pulled off the stalk.

He was close to my mother. She treated him like another son. One Saturday, I was helping Mama in the kitchen. She was cooking, getting ready for Camp Meeting the next day. Camp Meeting was a time when the churches would have a big picnic. They would have a preacher come for a revival. Everyone would bring food, and we would sing, enjoy fellowship, and have a great time.

Mama was known for her cooking—fried chicken, rolls, potato salad, and on and on. When we would go to Camp Meeting, she would always bring extra because she knew people would be coming to her to get some of her good food. But she was best known for her cakes—chocolate, caramel, coconut, and white-icing cake. I am an okay cook but never learned to do it like Mama.

We were in the kitchen sweating, cooking, and laughing when Howard ran in the front door all out of breath and said, "Mom, you'll never believe what just happened."

Mama and I both turned around at the same time and said, "What happened, Howard."

He went on to say what happened and then ran back outside. I don't even remember what it was; probably something the animals had done. He had called out, "Mom," and we both turned around. I didn't realize that he called my mother Mom too.

I was gone all day most days, and he was there with her and my brothers and sisters, who all called her Mom. So why wouldn't he call her Mom? I wasn't jealous and was happy that he loved her like a mother. But it still stung a little and reminded me how little time I got to spend with him.

I started with the BCD in January of 1943; little did I know that it would close soon. In August, Bituminous Coal Division and Solid Fuels combined, putting me out of a job. I had already resolved that I was not going back to washing diapers again. They gave us two weeks to find a new job without a break in service.

My supervisor had always looked out for me, and this was no different. She said to me, "Pearl, you live all the way up in Quince Orchard. You drive by the Navy medical hospital every day. Why don't you get a job there? I'll call and see if they'll hire you as one of their secretaries."

She called them, and yes, they had an opening. I was to report that Monday morning. I was excited about this new job, yet in the back of my mind, something was saying, *This isn't right.*

The Making of a Pearl

Monday morning, I go up to the office to start my job. As I entered the building, I recognized one of the janitors, Ed. He had grown up in Quince Orchard. We chatted for a little bit, and he asked me what I was doing there. I proudly told him that I was there to start my new job.

Ed chuckled, "Well, I'll be. What are you going to be doing? The only thing Black people do here is run the elevators and sweep the floors."

I laughed and said, "Not this time, my supervisor recommended me, and they already have a job for me in the secretary pool."

"Well, then, congratulations. Get on up there so you won't be late."

I felt like I could hear him shaking his head as I walked away and rode the elevator upstairs. I walked into the office to check in. I told them my name, and the woman behind the desk glanced up at me and then nodded at me to have a seat without saying a word. I sat down and waited. People came in and walked all around me, hanging up their coats. No one said anything to me.

Finally, I went up to the desk and said, "I am Ida Pearl Bell. I was supposed to report for work this morning at eight o'clock."

She said, "We don't have no job for you."

Ed downstairs had tried to warn me. But I just couldn't believe him. My supervisor from BCD told me that I already had the job.

"You must have a job for me. My supervisor told me that I had a job here and to report for work today. Can you please call her?" I gave her my office phone number, and she called my boss. I went and sat back down and smoothed out my skirt. I was confident that this would all get straightened out and I could start working. This seemed like a very nice place to work.

After they talked for a few minutes, she waved the phone at me without saying anything. I picked up the phone from her with a smile on my face.

My boss said, "Pearl, I am so sorry. I didn't know they don't hire colored people there."

With all the grace I could muster, I turned around and took the elevator back downstairs.

I saw Ed again in the lobby but just walked on by. I didn't want him to see me upset, and I figured he would know what happened. I caught the bus back to Rockville and then walked to meet Papa at the farm.

He looked at me as if to say why are you back so early. But he must have seen the disappointment on my face. He didn't ask me anything about the job. He just said, "Go on in the house and see what you can help with there. When I finish the afternoon chores, I'll take you back home." It may not have seemed like a lot, but I already knew Papa understood. He wasn't much for emotion, and neither was I. For him to be willing to take me home in the middle of the day, I knew he was just as upset as I was. We always tried to find the silver lining.

Eventually, my former boss found me a job as a file clerk at the Veterans Administration (VA). My first job was in the third basement. But it was a job, and I wasn't washing diapers. This was back in Washington, DC, and I had to get there by eight each morning. That meant Papa and I had a lot of early car rides, if we were lucky, or walking, if we weren't, to get to Rockville to catch the bus.

The third basement was a large dusty warehouse. It had files from the Civil War and the old wars. We had a ladder that we would push up and down the aisles to get files. It was hard work, and the conditions were very bad. When the weather turned cold, it seemed to get even worse. The secretary area was okay, but when we had to go back into the stacks and get files, it was cold and damp and smelled awful. They didn't have any heat in there.

I didn't realize it at first, but those conditions were awful for my foot. It started to ache and sometimes swell. I was glad that Papa's car was working more often, and we didn't have to make those long walks to Rockville as much. One day I was working, and I went to get up and go grab a file. I couldn't put any weight on my foot; it just ached so. I couldn't walk on it at all. I called home, and Papa drove out to the VA and carried me home. When I got there, Mama had a bucket of warm water ready for me to soak it in.

That was in December. I didn't go back to work until April. I felt like I spent the whole four months with my foot in that bucket of water. They said that arthritis had set in, I don't know what it was, but I couldn't walk. I was determined to walk again, though. Each day I would try a little bit, just a few steps, then a few more, and a few more. It was painstaking, I would lean on Mama, and she would help me around. I hated being a burden to everyone. I started making paper flowers again and sold them by the dozen to the churches.

At some point, I don't even know when, I started entertaining again. I would have friends over, and we would just talk and catch up. There wasn't really any place to go and sit like kids do now. We didn't have any bars or restaurants in Quince Orchard; you would have to go to Rockville for that. We just visited each other's homes. At twenty-six, I considered myself grown, a widow, and a working mom with a baby, but I never even considered the idea of living on my own.

I guess I could have found a place to live in Washington, DC, but it was good to have the support of my family. I always knew that little Howard would be taken care of. Even though he didn't have any siblings of his own, he could play with Esther like she was his sister. Of course, I still had to help out with the chores and with the little ones when I got home, but it was better than trying to manage a household completely on my own.

Living in my parents' house meant living by my parent's rules. Usually, I had no problems with being at home, but every now and then, I felt like I should be able to do adult things. Papa didn't allow anyone to drink alcohol in the house. One day, I decided I would be fancy and offer my friends a drink. I bought a bottle of Five Roses wine after leaving work one day and brought it home to share with my guests.

I put out glasses for them and poured a drink. Not long after I had poured the drinks, Mama came home. She walked by the parlor, looked at the drinks, looked at me, and then continued on to the kitchen. She didn't say anything, but that look was enough. I hurried them to finish their drinks, and then I ran upstairs and hid the bottle in the back of my closet. Decades later, it was still there. I never removed it, so I assume that when we tore the house down, the Five Roses bottle went with it.

Reflections on Life After Howard

World War II started in 1939, but the US didn't fully enter until December 1941. In June 1941, President Roosevelt issued an executive order forbidding discrimination in the employment of workers in the defense industry and in government because of race, creed, color, or national origin. Full desegregation of the federal workforce and military wouldn't come until President Truman in 1948. The war effort created jobs and helped to end the Great Depression. It also created new opportunities for women and African Americans to enter the workforce that didn't exist before.

While Grandma was certainly aware of the war, it felt distant. Aside from her brother's active-duty service, the war didn't touch her much. She and her family made the most of what they had and were rarely affected by the wartime rations. I doubt she was aware that the secretary test she took was an effort to get more women, even Black women, into the workforce to replace the men going off to war. She just saw it as an escape from the mundane life on the farm and an opportunity to stop domestic work.

Grandma's early years, when segregation wasn't as blatant, instilled in her a sense of belonging. She never had reason to fear White people and was never made to feel less than. She moved with a sense that she was supposed to be in this space, and when it was not granted to her, it was a flaw of the other person, not her. That changed as she ventured into the working world when the hard crush of segregation would be thrown into her face on multiple occasions.

While I have never been blatantly turned away from a job because of my race, as Grandma was, I can relate to the feeling of being made to feel like you don't belong. I recall one night in 2005 when my team was on call at the hospital. The ER called my colleague to admit a patient, a White male. When she arrived, he refused to be admitted because she was Black.

Both myself and the other intern, as well as our supervising residents, were all Black females. It just so happened that the hospitalist on call as well as the ER doctor working that night were all Black, and the patient refused to be admitted by any of us. He left the hospital against medical advice because he refused to be admitted by a Black physician.

At another time, a patient was convinced I was a nursing student despite my attending repeatedly telling her I was in medical school. Just about every Black doctor I know has a story of being mistaken for a food service worker or janitorial staff despite wearing professional attire, a white coat, and a badge labeled doctor.

In my grandmother's case, that firm community foundation helped her escape being crushed by the weight of segregation and gave her the courage and strength to press on. She was never one to be confrontational. You wouldn't find Grandma at a protest march or having ketchup poured on her at attempting to integrate a Woolworth's lunch counter. Buses in Washington, DC, were not segregated, so there was not much need for a bus boycott to protest being sent to the back of the bus.

The Civil Rights movement was still in its infancy in the 1940s. And unlike her brother Thompkins who became quite involved, Grandma focused on making a way for her family. She did not have time or energy for the grand movement. It is important to remember, though, that the Civil Rights movement required big and

The Making of a Pearl

small actions. And as Grandma's story will later show, these small, deliberate actions often result in lasting change just as much as the big showy ones.

Chapter 6
Mister Gerard

Mister Gerard

Gerard, on butchering day

Pearl and Gerard

The Making of a Pearl

> ¹*Praise the Lord. Blessed is the man who fears the Lord, who find great delight in his commands. ²His children will be mighty in the land; the generation of the upright will be blessed. ³Wealth and riches are in his house, and his righteousness endures forever... ⁶Surely he will never be shaken; a righteous man will be remembered forever.*
>
> Psalm 112:1-3, 6 (NIV)

After Howard died, I didn't want to see or talk to anyone. I definitely didn't want to even think about getting married again. It was all just too painful. First, my days were spent taking care of little Howard and my siblings while Mama and Papa worked. Then I started working, and with my long commute, it didn't leave much time for any socializing.

Throughout this time, I did find it helpful to talk to Gerard. He understood what it was like to lose a spouse and be a single parent. Sometimes he would come by and play with little Howard. Being the youngest in his family, Gerard had never really been around babies. When he held Howard for the first time, he didn't know what to do; he just stood there with his arms outstretched, holding him at arm's length.

Howard just loved to see Mr. Gerard come by. He would get down on the floor and play with him. One day when he was about four, Howard said to me, "Mother, can you marry Mr. Gerard so he can be my father."

Gerard and I got married in September of 1948. I was thirty. We went to the justice of the peace in Clarksburg, just Gerard, Howard, and me. Esther was upset that she couldn't go because she was used to going with us on all our outings. It turns out Gerard purchased property and started building a house on Quince Orchard Road before we even started courting. He wanted a nice house for himself, a step up from the one he grew up in, which is where he was living. Gerard wanted something that was all his own, without being haunted by ghosts of his childhood.

While he built the house for himself, it was beautiful and just perfect for the three of us—his stepdaughter, Helen, was already married with a family of her own. The new house wasn't quite ready at the time of our wedding, so I continued to live with my parents until the house was finished that November.

It was bigger than most of the other houses he built. It had two stories with electricity and running water in the kitchen. When we first moved in, there weren't any bathrooms, and we had to use the outhouse. That took some getting used to, especially for little Howard, as my parents had already gotten indoor bathrooms. Bathrooms came soon after we moved in.

There were four rooms downstairs and two bedrooms upstairs, plus a basement. We loved to host everyone at our house. We had a television, and all the family would come over to watch it on the weekends. They would squeeze into our tiny living room and watch the small television screen. It didn't seem small at the time, nor did it feel crowded. Those were happy days with family around. We didn't have much, but we were thankful for everything we had.

With just the three of us, it certainly was a lot quieter than what little Howard and I were used to. I gave Howard the choice of coming to live with Gerard and me or staying with my parents. He chose to come live with us. We would drop him off at Mama's in the morning on our way out to work. He would eat breakfast there and catch the bus to school. He'd go back there after school, and Gerard would pick him up on his way home after work. Gerard would usually get supper ready since I wouldn't get back home until after six o'clock in the evening.

Gerard loved children. It made him happy to see them happy. Maybe because he never had much of a childhood of his own. At Halloween, he would put hay in the big wagon, hook it up to the tractor and take the kids around the neighborhood for trick-or-treating. They would line up at Snyder's Store for candy. Mr. Snyder would always tell the little ones to get in front so he could make sure they got something in case he ran out. But he never ran out of candy. Gerard would tease the children by taking his teeth out and giving them a gummy grin. Some thought it funny; others would run screaming.

He went to the dentist to get his teeth pulled and fitted for false teeth. He went in and was fitted for his upper dentures, and he was told to return a couple weeks later to get the bottoms. Well, between appointments, the dentist died. There weren't many other dentists in the area who would see Black patients. And by the time there was a new dentist, he was used to not having any bottom teeth. Once his

The Making of a Pearl

gums got hard, it didn't slow him down any. His favorite snack was chomping on dry roasted peanuts.

Gerard worked as an exterminator and janitor at the National Institutes of Health (NIH) in Bethesda. It was a good job with the government. Initially, he worked during the day until he had a falling out with his boss, and then he was moved to nights. I never quite knew what happened, but I imagine his temper must have gotten the best of him. At first, it was a setback, but God turned it into a positive. With him working nights, he could be around during the day to help with the kids. It also gave him time to do his carpentry work and farming, which brought in extra money for the family.

At NIH, he developed a fear of elevators. On more than one occasion, he got stuck in an elevator. After that, he always took the stairs until he was too old and sick to do it. He didn't like boats or airplanes either. He preferred to have his feet firmly planted on the ground.

Our little house on Quince Orchard Road was filled with love. While on the outside, one might consider us poor, we never felt that way. We always had plenty to eat. Gerard had a small farm down the road with a few pigs and cows. In our yard, he kept turkeys—in cages so they never touched the ground—and we always had a garden. Most of our food we grew on our own, and we bought the basics like flour, sugar, salt, and pepper from Snyder's Store up the street, just like I did when I was younger. Butchering always brought in a bit of extra money too.

At Thanksgiving time, Gerard would string up turkeys on the swing we had in the back and then cut off their heads. Once, one got loose and ran all over the backyard without its head until it flopped down dead. I would remove the feathers, scald the birds, and prepare them to sell. We would take them all around Quince Orchard to sell for Thanksgiving. While butchering turkeys was done by Gerard and me, and the boys once they got older, butchering the pigs seemed to get the whole community involved.

Gerard would choose a cold weekend day for the butchering. Men from all around would come to help, and the boys would be there too. He would kill the pigs on the farm, load them on the back of his truck and take them to have the entrails removed. Then he would bring them back and take them to the shed in the backyard to do the butchering.

My cousin Emma and I would be inside, and they would bring us the scraps to make sausage, and we would use the lard to make soap.

Hams were salted and hung up in the barn to cure. We would always bring out a salted ham on special occasions like Thanksgiving and Christmas. Gerard would take the meat and sell it at his job at NIH. It was good food and good money. But most of all, it brought the community together.

Reflections on Mister Gerard

Gerard Americus Green, Grandpa Green to me, was born on November 21, 1909, in Darnestown, MD, the next town up the road from Quince Orchard. Grandpa's father, Vernon Green, was born into slavery in 1858 and freed along with his siblings and his parents, Gary and Matilda Green, during the Maryland emancipation of 1864.

Vernon married Sadie Murray around 1900. Gerard was the youngest of their four sons, Douglas, Carroll, Arthur, and Gerard. He would have been the second youngest, but his mother and would-be sibling died in childbirth. His father soon remarried, but his stepmother was not fond of Gerard or any of his brothers.

Grandpa's father sharecropped on the farms of others. His father and his father before him were also good with their hands and worked as carpenters. There were some happy times, like Christmas and Santa Claus, before his brother ruined that. One year Douglas announced at dinner there was no Santa Claus. Grandpa's father got so angry that he slapped him, but then he said to Arthur and Grandpa, "Well, I guess you know the truth now. There won't be a Santa Claus this year."

His childhood was hard, filled with lots of work. They earned extra money from cutting and shucking corn and used that to get Christmas gifts. Their father always got them clothes, and their grandmother made nightgowns out of feed sacks.

Before school, he would feed the chickens while his brothers fed the pigs and horses. After school, they would feed the animals again and gather wood for the stove. Grandpa also attended the Quince Orchard Colored School. And while Grandma's schooling was interrupted by problems with her foot and helping to raise her siblings, Grandpa's was interrupted by the need to work and help support his family.

Starting from a young age, he and his brothers had to work to harvest feed corn. When the harvest was done in December, then

The Making of a Pearl

they could start school. He would also have to end his school year early, before April, to help with the spring planting.

Two of his brothers were able to go all the way through the seventh grade, which was the last grade offered at Quince Orchard Colored School. When Grandpa went to school, he spent a lot of time catching up on what he missed and often stayed inside over recess to practice his studies. He stopped going after the third or fourth grade upon the death of his father.

When Grandpa was nine, his father, a carpenter, fell off a roof and died. He and his brothers stayed with his stepmother for a while, but it wasn't long before she put them out to work on the farms of White families nearby. Grandpa worked on the farm of Roy Darby; they paid a quarter per day for milking cows and helping with odd jobs. He would receive a payment of $7.50 at the end of the month and bring that back to the family.

He was also raised at Pleasant View church, where my grandmother attended. His grandfather, the same Gary Green, helped purchase and build both the school and the church. Gerard was always dedicated to preserving and protecting that property and later became the chairman of the Pleasant View Historical Association.

Grandpa was nine years older than Grandma, but they lived in the same community. He worked as a carpenter, much like his father and grandfather before him. He was always good with his hands. Even in the years he worked at Navy Medical and the National Institutes of Health, he kept his carpentry skills.

He built many of the houses and barns in the Quince Orchard area. He saw it as his gift to the community. He didn't charge much, only enough to cover the materials costs and a little extra for him. It created a sense of pride for Blacks to own land and a house, and he was proud to help more people attain that.

It is not a secret that my grandparents were cousins. Gary and Matilda Green were my grandfather's grandparents, my grandmother's great-grandparents. Lucky for us, their gene pool was distinct enough that their kids had no birth defects. It was not uncommon in those days to marry a distant cousin; the communities were so small it was hard not to.

Despite my grandfather's father being born into slavery, my grandmother claims not to have known of slavery in the area. Slavery was not talked about, not even whispered about. The story of Gary Green and his friends purchasing land and building a church and schoolhouse was proudly passed down through generations. However, the piece about him being enslaved was not. When I was younger, I asked my grandmother if any of our ancestors were enslaved.

She replied that there was no slavery in this area. She was not lying or trying to protect me; our family's slave story was never told to her. Later, upon sharing the history that we had discovered, she reasoned it had been kept from her because slavery was just too painful to talk about. My grandparents and their parent's before them, carried a legacy of shame related to slavery that they did not want to be associated with. They saw themselves as distinct from Africa and were quick to distinguish themselves from more recently immigrated Africans.

Grandma and her sisters love to travel, but anywhere in Africa is a quick no on the places they want to visit. Most of the stories about Africans in those days showed uneducated people in destitute poverty with little clothing and bloated bellies. That was something that they did not want to be associated with. My grandmother's generation felt the need to show White people and the world that they were more sophisticated, could work as peers, and belonged in America.

My parents' generation started to reclaim our connections to Africa. Many chose African or uniquely Black names, like Kisha. My parents have been to Zimbabwe three times, once with my sister and me. I studied abroad in Ghana, and my brother studied in South Africa. And yet none of our stories or pictures could reassure Grandma that this was a place worth visiting. Her early imprinting was just too strong.

Bunny Heller, a family friend, recorded a series of interviews with Grandpa when his health started failing. In one, she asks him what he wishes for his grandchildren. I paused the recording and turned it up so I could intently listen to what he desired for my life. Simply put, he said he wanted us to have the opportunity to choose to do whatever we wanted. At first, I was disappointed. That's it? He doesn't want us to go to college, get a professional degree, or have a family? But what he wanted for us was something that he didn't have as a child—the ability to choose our own path.

Chapter 7
Starting a Family Again

Starting a Family Again

The Green Family

Back row: Gerard, Pearl, Howard, Front row: Peaches, Vernon

The Making of a Pearl

> [3]*Children are a heritage from the Lord, offspring a reward from him. [4]Like arrows in the hands of a warrior are children born in one's youth. [5]Blessed is the man whose quiver is full of them.*
>
> *Psalm 127:3-5a (NIV)*

Gerard and I were happy in our new house. He was working at the NIH, and I was working at the VA downtown. When I told him I was pregnant, I thought he would pop because he puffed his chest out so proud.

His stepdaughter Helen was now married to Charles Thompson, and they already had three children of their own. We had grandchildren before Gerard had any kids of his own. Of course, Howard called him Daddy because he was the only father he had ever really known. Gerard loved both Helen and Howard, but he was so excited to be having a child of his own.

He was excited, but I was worried. I was worried about losing Gerard or the baby. I got worried whenever we got into a car. And I was scared to dream. Anytime I was sleeping and even started to dream, I would wake myself up. If something bad was going to happen this time, I didn't want to know.

We were blessed that everything went smoothly. The new baby arrived in November of 1950, just one week after Gerard's birthday, we named him Gerard Americus Green, Jr., but we called him Peaches because he was covered with what looked like peach fuzz when he was born.

I spent the winter at home with Peaches. I was supposed to go back to work in April. I showed up on my first day back, worked one day, and gave my resignation. From that day, like my mother did when I was born, I became mostly a mother.

After Peaches was born, I started selling Fashion Frock dress patterns. Even though I wasn't going to work every day, I always thought it was important to do something to bring in extra money. Mama's lessons of always having your own money and her knack for selling things were instilled in me. I was a good seller, and when I would sell a certain number, I would get a free dress.

I earned lots of free dresses, and that made me feel like one of the most fashionable ladies in the neighborhood. I also took in cleaning and sewing and helped watch other kids in the neighborhood. I appreciated the extra money it brought into the house. Gerard was working nights at NIH and doing construction jobs during the day. It was a busy time for us.

Vernon arrived on January 1, 1955, the first baby born in the county that year. I figured this would be my last baby. I was thirty-six, and Gerard was forty-five. Even though my mother had Esther when she was over forty, I didn't think I would have a child that late in life. I don't know how Mama did it with eight children. My three boys seemed plenty to handle. I also helped to care for Helen's kids. They would stay with us during the day while their parents worked.

I enjoyed selling Fashion Frocks because I liked giving women something to help them feel beautiful. But once Vernon came, I had to stop because selling took up so much time. In 1958 I heard about Avon, and I loved the idea of becoming an Avon lady. I got signed up and started going to the meetings.

I was the only Black woman there, the first one to join that unit. I didn't let that stop me or slow me down. I would come into the meetings and sit right on the first row. When I started, my manager told me that I was only to sell in the Black neighborhoods and not to overlap with any of the territories that the other White sellers had. Well, I went to Lincoln Park and Quince Orchard and told everyone I knew about Avon. Before I knew it, I was one of the top sellers.

One evening my manager pulled me aside and said, "Pearl, the other ladies are concerned that you must be going into their territories to sell since you are doing so well."

I stood up tall, put my shoulder's back, and said, "No, I'm staying in my territory, Lincoln Park and Quince Orchard. Black women want to look beautiful just as much as anybody else."

Selling Fashion Frocks and later Avon allowed me to be home with Peaches and Vernon when they were young. Avon also gave me the motivation to start driving again.

One time, not long after Howard passed, Papa asked me to go get something from the store and come home. It was only a mile drive each way. I made it to the store okay, but on the way back, I couldn't breathe. I started to sweat, and my heart was racing. First I was hot, but then a cold chill started. I was gripping the steering wheel with all my strength, and I felt like I couldn't see. I was just creeping along in the car, and any time anything went by, I felt like I was going to jump out of my skin.

Papa saw me coming down the lane; he must have wondered why I was going so slow. To me, it felt like I was going a hundred miles an

The Making of a Pearl

hour, and at the same time, it felt like I was never going to make it home. He met me at the car and opened the door. I practically fell out; I was sweating and crying. He held me and said, "It's okay, Pearl. I won't make you drive anymore." I wiped my tears, went into the house, and lay down.

When I started selling Avon in 1958, Gerard would have to take me everywhere. We would go to the post office to pick up my order and then go to my cousin Emma's house in Rockville to sack it all up. Then I would walk all over Lincoln Park to deliver it. He would drive me to places that were far or if my foot was bothering me. Then we would get back home in the evening. We would spend the better part of a day doing that every other weekend.

I think Gerard was getting tired of losing his Saturdays to Avon, so he said, "Pearl, why don't you start driving again? Then you can carry yourself to Rockville or wherever else you need to go. You can also take the kids places when I'm at work."

I was hesitant at first, but it had been almost twenty years since Howard died.

The first time I sat behind the wheel after Gerard encouraged me, I started to feel the hot sweats and cold chills. My heart started racing, and my vision narrowed, just like the last time. But then I stopped, and I prayed. And I said to myself, "Pearl, you can do this." My breathing slowed, and my vision came into focus. I was nervous at first, but pretty soon, it all came back to me. And once I started driving again, you couldn't stop me. I liked having my independence back to go where I wanted when I wanted without having to depend on someone for a ride.

I was often the one giving other people a ride and helping them get places they needed to go. I felt like Papa, though I didn't ask for gas money from everyone like he did. From then until I stopped driving at the age of ninety-two, I would always do the same thing. I would get in, turn the ignition, and count to one hundred to make sure the car was good and running. In my counting was a prayer to keep me safe. God was with me every time. I never was in another car accident.

Just because I was driving again didn't mean I had all my independence. One time I was going to Rockville to do my Avon, and I needed gas. I got gas, paid, and then left my car at the gas station since it was close to the start of the neighborhood. I spent the whole afternoon into the early evening walking through Lincoln Park, delivering Avon, and talking to people. When I got back to the car, I couldn't find my keys. I looked all through my purse, and I worried that maybe I left them at someone's house while I was visiting.

As I expected, the gas station was closed, so I had to go to a neighbor to call Gerard to bring me the extra set. He teased me when he picked me up, "So, you want to drive, but you don't have keys. How is Ms. Avon going to get to all her customers?"

Two weeks later, I went back to Rockville to do it all over again and stopped at the same gas station to get gas. When I went inside, the owner asked, "Are these your keys? You left them on the counter when you came in a couple of weeks ago. We held them here for you, but you never came back until today."

I felt so dumb but was so glad God was looking out for me. When I got home that evening, I took the spare keys and hung them on the key hook at home. When Gerard got home, I saw him look at the keys, look at me, and he never said another word about it.

Peaches started kindergarten at Rock Terrace elementary school. The Quince Orchard Colored School where I had gone closed in the 1940s. My older son Howard went there for one year before it closed.

All the kids in all grades from the neighborhood took the same bus to school. The bus would start up in Seneca and then come down to Quince Orchard and go on to Rockville. It would drop the high school students off at Carver, the junior high kids at Lincoln Park, and the elementary students at Rock Terrace. While these schools were newer than what I went to, they were still only for colored children. The bus ride was about an hour each way.

Peaches did not like school. Every morning when it was time to walk out to the bus stop, he would start crying. Howard would take him by the hand and lead him out to the bus stop. "Come on, Peaches; you'll be fine. Stop crying."

One of his teachers, Mrs. Annie Rhodes, knew how to get him to stop crying. One day she heard that he cried every day on the way to school. She called him in and said, "I hear you are crying because you don't want to go to school. School is your ticket to something better, so you should learn to love it." Then she spanked him with a ruler and told him, "That will give you something to cry about."

It must have worked; he didn't cry about school again, and he loved school from there on out. He went on to college and earned three master's degrees and his Ph.D.

When Peaches started kindergarten in 1955, schools were still segregated, but that soon changed. They built a new integrated school called Travilah, and everyone would start there together. The school

The Making of a Pearl

opened in 1959, and he went for fifth grade. His cousin Melvin Joppy started there along with them.

Peaches and his friends adjusted to the new school and new kids just fine. Most of them knew each other and played together since we were all on the same street. It was great that the school was so much closer than before, only a fifteen-minute bus ride instead of the hour it took before. And the school was just for kids his own age, not all the junior and high school kids. Vernon attended integrated schools from when he started kindergarten. And for him, his activities out of school were integrated, too, starting with Cub Scouts.

Vernon's first Cub Scout troop was all Black, and we had to go all the way down to Rockville at the church to meet. But then they started an integrated troop by us. I was one of the co-leaders and would drive Vernon and Bobby Joppy, and Arthur Green, Jr. to the meetings. We met at a big home in Darnestown. The White kids in that group were so troublesome.

At every meeting, one boy would run off and hide in the woods, and someone would have to go look for him. Other White boys would jump off the furniture, yell, and just be crazy. On the drives back home, I always told our boys that they were never to act like that. It didn't matter that they saw the White boys behaving that way; if I ever saw them acting like that, I'd beat them right then.

Peaches and Vernon got to do activities and got some spoiling that Howard never had, partly because I was just a single mom when Howard was little and didn't have time or money for the extras. And partly because Gerard didn't believe in spoiling Howard. One year a week or so before Easter, Gerard came home smiling.

He excitedly called Peaches and Vernon into the little room. He didn't call Howard, but he came anyway. Gerard pulled two new store-bought suits out of the bag, just bursting with pride, and urged the boys to go try them on. There was nothing for Howard in that bag, and I could see the disappointment on his face. He didn't say anything, just turned and walked out of the room.

I angrily turned to Gerard. "Why nothing for Howard?"

Gerard just said, "He already has a suit he can wear for Easter."

I'm not one to argue, and I didn't want Howard to feel bad. I went to my Avon money and took myself right to the store to get him a new suit as well. On Easter morning, when they all came down in their new suits, Gerard just glared at me. I knew he would say something later about me giving Howard too much or coddling him, but I didn't care. That morning we all looked beautiful for Easter service.

My mother was always quick with discipline, usually spankings. I was too, but I didn't have to do it as much. As soon as the boys were big enough, they went with their father to help him build houses, tend the animals, or whatever other odd job he might be doing. Since they were with them more, he did most of the disciplining. Back then, it was a close-knit community, and your neighbors would be sure to tell you if your child was doing wrong before they even got home.

One afternoon Peaches was playing with some kids by a tree that had fallen over by a mailbox. Someone came and told me that he had been playing in the mailboxes, messing with other people's mail. When he got home, I was waiting for him with a switch. He got quite a beating. All throughout, he was yelling, "I didn't do it. I wasn't playing in the mailbox. I was just climbing the tree. Somebody else was in the mail."

After he was done crying, I told him, "It doesn't matter whether or not you were the one messing with the mail. If you are hanging with a crowd that is getting into trouble, then you are going to be included in that. Don't hang with a gang that is not doing what they are supposed to."

To this day, he still gives me a hard time for getting that beating because he swears he wasn't doing anything wrong. And I stand by it because it taught him to be careful of who he keeps company with.

Reflections on Starting a Family Again

The Brown v. Board of Education decision to desegregate came in 1954, and it came to Montgomery County not long after. By the spring of 1955, the county had developed a three-year implementation plan starting with redrawing boundaries so children could attend the school closest to them. In the fall of 1955, four substandard Negro schools closed, and those students were reassigned to all-White schools at the elementary, junior, and high school levels.

Throughout that school year, the county set about educating teachers, students, and parents on integration through community forums, meetings, and fact sheets. It is not known how much of this was geared to the African American communities. Grandma does not remember anyone coming to talk to the Quince Orchard community about integrating schools.

While all of this was going on, she was becoming a mother yet again. Vernon was born on January 1st, 1955, and keeping house

The Making of a Pearl

while caring for a new infant, getting Peaches ready for school, and Howard starting high school did not leave much time for civic engagement. But the world around her and Quince Orchard was changing.

My father, Peaches, attended Rock Terrace Elementary from kindergarten through fourth grade, along with other Black students from the upper part of the county. Then the county built a new school, Travilah Elementary School, that would open completely integrated, which was ideal because no one could claim the school as theirs or refer back to how the school "used to be." A fresh start with a new experiment in integration. The school was ready that fall, and after Christmas vacation, Black kids and White kids started together in a brand new school with brand new materials to start a brand new chapter.

The Quince Orchard area, even going back to my grandmother's youth, was a mix of Black and White families. When my grandmother attended school, several of the Black communities in the county had their own one-room schoolhouses. However, by the time my father started school, the smaller community schools had closed, and all the Blacks were bused to a larger segregated school for kids from across the upper portion of the county. The desegregation of schools actually brought him closer to the reality that he saw in his neighborhood.

My family still lives in the Quince Orchard area. My brother and I both attended Travilah and later were part of the first class of students to attend a new elementary school, Jones Lane, where my children also attended. The school continues to be quite diverse. One of my favorite nights of the school year is World Culture Night, where families set up booths representing their cultural heritage. Last year there were over thirty countries represented from all over the world. It is a blessing to grow up in a place with such diversity.

My kids have grown up with friends of many different races from many cultures. This is important to me. The area was pretty diverse when I went to school and has grown even more so since then. It wasn't until I went to college that I realized how rare it was to have that level of diversity and integration. In college, I met White people who had never had a real conversation with a Black person, let alone had a sleepover at their house, and the same was true for many of my Black classmates.

While my children have grown up in an integrated world, I recognize that I must also prepare them for the harsh reality outside *of our bubble. Black boys don't always get to act like little boys. That was true when my dad grew up and is still true today. I teach them that someone is always watching. That is in part true because when you grow up in the same neighborhood as your parents, grandparents, and great-grandparents, someone always knows who you are. But also, because, as Black boys, they stand out in the crowd.*

My middle son is the tallest in his class, with beautiful hazel eyes that make him distinctive. He is often marked as guilty by association because he easily stands out when he is in a group. He has to understand that even when he is doing right, if his friends around him are doing wrong, he may get blamed. That is true now, just like it was for his grandfather decades earlier. But the consequences now—in a society quick to jump to guns and police who often escalate—make it even more worrisome. This is the reality for which I must prepare my children.

Chapter 8
Howard's Coming of Age

Vernon, Gerard, Howard, and Peaches pose for Easter Sunday

The Making of a Pearl

> [12] *I know what it is to have little, and I know what it is to have plenty. In any and all circumstances I have learned the secret of being well-fed and of going hungry, of having plenty and of being in need.* [13] *I can do all things through him who strengthens me.*
>
> Philippians 4:12-13 (NRSV)

Our family was growing and changing all the time. Little Howard grew up so fast. Before we knew it, he was in high school and working on the side. He tried out for football but preferred working and making extra money instead. He always had a side job; I guess he gets that from me. He did different odd jobs—cleaning houses and keeping up yards.

A lawyer he worked for in Rockville for quite some time paid him well. One day Howard came home, and I heard him in the yard just banging things around and making noise. He storms into the house, and his face is hardened, and he's stomping around.

"What's gotten into you," I say.

"Nothing; its nothing."

"Well, clearly, it's something, or you wouldn't be knocking and banging all around the house."

"I just need to find a new job, that's all. Mister doesn't need me anymore."

"Oh, why not?"

"I don't know. Certainly isn't for any good reason."

"Oh, so nothing happened?"

"No"

"No, nothing at all?"

"No, nothing at all. He just doesn't like Black people."

"Howard, what happened? You've been working for him for months and always said he was nice to you and paid you well. So what changed?"

After a pause, he said, "Today, I was finishing up, and I had to go to the bathroom. I had to go so bad, and I couldn't hold it until I got back home. So, I used the toilet in his house. I cleaned it after I was done, but he must have heard me passing urine. When I finished and opened the door, he was standing there, and his face looked like fire. He was so mad. He said, 'Boy, how dare you use the bathroom in the house. Don't you have any home training? Colored boys don't use bathrooms in this house. If that is how you are going to treat me and my family, then there is no need in you coming back ever again.' I just said, 'Yes, sir, and left.' Mama, I just don't understand. Did he want me to pee on his roses? I tried to hold it as long as I could. Where would I go other than in the bathroom?"

"I'm sorry, Howard. Some people carry a lot of hate in their hearts. But you shouldn't hate him for it. God forgive them, for they know not what they do. You need to pray for him."

I don't know if Howard ever prayed for that man, but I certainly did. It hurt me to see him so upset, but I also knew it wouldn't be the last time he felt that way.

Every day after school, Howard was off to one of his jobs. Arthur, Gerard's brother, put the idea of a car in his head. Arthur came to Gerard and said, "You know, with all of these jobs Howard has, he should get his license. That way, he won't have to depend on you or the bus for rides to get there."

Gerard replied, "Humph, well, I don't know how he's going to do that. It certainly won't be in my car." Later that evening at dinner, Gerard looked at Howard and said, "Arthur tells me he thinks you should learn how to drive."

Howard played dumb like he didn't know what Gerard was talking about, but I knew that Arthur didn't come up with this idea all on his own. "Well, Dad, I don't know what Uncle Arthur is talking about. But it would be easier for me to get to work after school if I could drive. I could even take you to work. I would make sure there is always gas in the car."

"You can get your license, but you won't be driving my car. You will need to get your own car and pay for your own insurance."

I don't think Howard heard anything after Gerard said you can get your license. His eyes just lit up, and he tried to hide this silly grin that extended from ear to ear.

A week later, Gerard comes home towing this beat-up 51 Ford and puts it in the yard. It was just a mess. The seats were all torn up; it was scratched on the side, and it didn't even run. He told Howard, "I found this car and paid twenty-five dollars for it, so you owe me twenty-five dollars." I guess Gerard liked the idea of Howard being able to take himself to work and start getting around on his own.

Every weekend he and Gerard were out in the yard working on that car. Howard would get paid and give $5 to Gerard each week until the car was paid off, and then he would buy things for the car. He got new black and red seat covers, and Gerard bought him some car paint for the outside. When Gerard was gone to work, Howard would use Gerard's car to practice in our driveway. I never mentioned that to Gerard. They finally got Howard's car running, and Howard taught himself to drive.

Howard went and got his license; I think the first time he parallel parked was when he went out for his license. He was so proud, and I think Gerard was proud of him too. He was the only one of his friends with his own car. Now he could drive himself to school instead of taking the hour-long bus ride. He was so proud to be able to take his date to prom in his own car. He was dressed up in a suit and went off to go pick her up. About fifteen minutes later here, he comes walking back into the house.

Gerard said, "What are you doing back so soon? Did you forget something?"

Howard's face was fallen, and he said, "No, my car broke down at the end of the street."

Gerard came to his rescue. "Well, since it is your prom and you are on your way to pick up your date, you can use my car just this once."

"Dad, thank you, thank you, thank you!" He grabbed the keys and took off.

"Don't burn out the clutch," Gerard yelled after him chuckling. Gerard walked down to Howard's car at the end of the lane. He fooled around with it, got it running again, and drove it home. He walked in, just chuckling to himself. "All it needed was a little oil; he just didn't want to get his shirt dirty."

We were so thankful when Howard graduated from high school. Sometimes we weren't sure he would graduate because his grades were so bad. But he made it through. I asked him if he wanted to go to college. I told him that if he did, I would go back to work to help pay for it. He told me, "No, Mother, I'm going to work and help take care of you."

A couple of years after he graduated high school, he entered military service. Papa and I had gone with each of my brothers to see them off when they entered the army. Now it was my turn to do the same for my own son. Now I understood why Mama never wanted to go. But I had to go and see him off.

He was dressed in his uniform and looked just so dapper. He volunteered to go to Vietnam because he wanted the extra money. But God stepped in. After his basic training in Georgia, he was sent to France. Once they realized his skills as a clerk, he was kept in

France because they didn't need clerks in Vietnam. I was so thankful that he never had to go to Vietnam. I prayed for him constantly.

The day after he arrived in France, we got the awful news of the assassination of President Kennedy. I was so worried for Howard. If they could do that to the President of the United States, what could they do to soldiers like my son in a foreign country?

He would send letters home on red-lined paper, the same as my brothers before him. He told us of his travels to Spain, Denmark, Sweden, and all over the rest of Europe.

While Howard was away, we settled into a new routine of just the four of us. Peaches was in junior high, and Vernon was in elementary. I started having trouble with my foot again; my toes had curled under. The doctor said I needed surgery to straighten them so my foot wouldn't ball up any more than it already had. I went into surgery that Friday feeling just fine, happy even. They put pins in the toes to make them straight. Afterward, it seemed like everything went well. I had a good conversation with my hospital roommate that evening. Gerard was at home watching the boys.

Around midnight the night of the surgery, the nurse came in and said I had a fever. She called the doctor. He came and looked and started poking and prodding my toes. They whisked me off to a private room. I didn't know what was happening, and it didn't seem like they did either. One of the toes was infected, and they had to take it off. I started praying. I prayed all night. Saturday morning, the doctor comes in, lifts up the sheet, looks at my foot, frowns, shakes his head, and just walks right back out. He didn't say anything to me, but I heard him talking in the hallway to the nurse.

He says, "We'll watch it another day, but if the infection doesn't clear, we will probably have to cut it off." I just kept praying. On Sunday morning, the doctor came in real early. He pulled back the sheet again and looked at my foot. He pokes at it some. He looked surprised. Then he turns to me and says, "Mrs. Green, would you like to go home today?"

I sat up and said, "Well, yes. Since it's Sunday, you have to call my husband now before he leaves for church. Tell him to take the kids on to Sunday school and then come get me. My mother can bring them home from church."

Gerard came and picked me up, and I was home by supper time. Here again, they were ready to cut my foot, and prayer brought me through. This wasn't the last time my foot caused me trouble. Like a

The Making of a Pearl

cicada, every fifteen to twenty years, foot trouble seemed to come back to remind me to put my faith in God.

Howard served his two years and then came home. We were glad to see him back safe. So many others came back injured or didn't come home at all.

Much had changed in those two years while he was gone. For one, his girlfriend, Barbara, whom he had planned to marry, was now pregnant. I think he still loved her and was broken-hearted that she hadn't waited for him. She wasn't married, though, and no one seemed to know who the father was, so he thought he still had a chance.

He went to Gerard for advice. I think he was expecting Gerard to encourage him to follow his heart. Gerard had raised two children that weren't his own. Gerard told him he shouldn't saddle himself down with raising what isn't his. That always left me to wonder, is that how he really felt about Helen and Howard? Saddled down and burdened by their existence?

After Howard returned, he lived back with us and started working at the grocery store. He was now twenty-five and felt big for our little house. He and Gerard were bumping heads more and more. Howard wanted to stay out late. He knew better than to bring girls home, but sometimes he was trying to sneak in before Gerard got in from work or wouldn't come in altogether. I didn't like him going out so much, but I loved having all my sons there with me.

Gerard thought otherwise. "Pearl, he's a grown man now. It's time for him to go."

"Yes, but he can stay here. I'll talk to him about coming in earlier."

"No," Gerard said. "He needs to be in his own place so he can grow up. At his age, if he wants to stay out and party, he can do that. But he can't do it here. Peaches and Vernon don't need to see him sneaking around with women or drinking and partying. He finished school, and he's been in the army, gone overseas, and now been back home for over a year. He needs to grow up and learn to provide for himself."

I didn't say anything more. I prayed for Gerard's heart to soften. I prayed for Howard to do better.

That was the end of it, at least for a while. We didn't talk about it again until one morning at breakfast. I got all of the food on the table—scrapple, eggs, and toast. We said grace, and everyone was digging into the food like usual. Peaches and Vernon were bickering about some silly thing, poking and kicking each other under the table.

Then Gerard stopped, sat up a little straighter, smoothed the napkin in his lap, and cleared his throat. I looked at him as if to say, what is this all about? The boys didn't even notice and kept right on bickering and eating.

After clearing his throat again, he said, "Howard, you've been here long enough. It's time for you to get your own place. You have until the end of the month. Two weeks should be enough time for you to find something." Then he picked up his fork and went back to eating like nothing had happened.

Everyone else sat there stunned. Peaches and Vernon looked at each other, then from Gerard to Howard and Howard to Gerard, and then to me with eyes as big as saucers, but they didn't make a peep.

Howard pushed away from the table, threw down his napkin, and said, "So you are just going to kick me out?" He stormed outside, and I stood up to go after him.

Gerard said, "Pearl, sit down. He'll be okay. Boys, stop staring; eat your food."

We all ate silently, just the sound of our folks and knives scraping the plates. I was holding back tears but knew this wasn't a time for crying.

Then Vernon says, "Well, can I get his bed?"

Peaches fires back, "Of course not. I'm the next oldest. His bed is mine. You wouldn't be able to keep it clean anyway."

Gerard somberly said, "Boys, finish your food."

Later that evening, when Howard returned home after work, I went and sat with him in his room. He said, "Mother, doesn't Daddy love me?"

"Of course he does."

"Then why is Daddy kicking me out? He wouldn't make Peaches or Vernon leave."

"Howard, you are a grown man now. You need your own space to be responsible for. If you want to go out, you are old enough to do that, but you can't do that and stay here. Daddy and I love you, and that is why it is time for you to move out."

Howard moved to a rooming house in Washington, DC, and later found his own apartment in the city. When I had some extra money, I would send it to him, but I wouldn't tell Gerard.

Reflections on Howard's Coming of Age

As Howard came of age, Grandma's foot reared its ugly head yet again. Like previously, her interactions with the healthcare community are harsh and matter-of-fact. Little compassion is given for the potential impact that cutting off part of her foot would bring. And when healed, likely due to the miracle of antibiotics that were now in regular supply, she is dismissed.

I wish I could say that the medical community has improved in the compassion and care that it shows to its patients. We have not. A recent article showed that ChatGPT, a natural language processing tool, gave more compassionate and empathetic answers to medical questions than doctors did. Disappointingly, I'm not surprised.

My dad always looked up to his big brother Howard. He was always the cool one with fancy clothes, a nice car, and a beautiful girl on his arm. Howard bought Dad his first car, though Grandpa wouldn't let him drive it.

By the time I arrived on the scene, he had two sons, Kevin and Tim, ten and nine years older than me, respectively. They lived with their mother, but she and Uncle Howard never married. My older cousins would ride their dirt bikes at our house and visit my mom for math tutoring. I still have a scar on my knee from a trip through the woods riding on the seat behind Tim on that dirt bike.

What I think my dad admired most about Uncle Howard was how he handled himself. He had an easy way with people and always seemed comfortable in any group. The strong silent type not easily flustered—except for when his car broke down on prom night. A protector who guided dad on the bus in kindergarten and looked out for them as they grew older. Dad watched as Howard was treated differently by their father and marveled at his resilience. I'd say Howard got that from his mother.

I remember stories and pictures of Howard's first wife, Aunt Kathleen. I don't remember much of her other than her voice, sweet with an island accent. Grandma tells of the wonderful trip they took to visit her family in Trinidad—absent Grandpa, of course, since he didn't like planes or water. It was Grandma's first time out of the country and sparked a travel bug that lived for decades.

Howard getting kicked out had a big impact on him as well as my father. My father says it affected him so much that he promised himself he would leave before Grandpa could kick him out.

Grandma, however, says she barely remembers it; she tends to minimize the hard stuff.

What was never clear to me was why Grandpa asked him to leave so abruptly. Grandma said Howard was getting too old, and too many men were in the house. Howard would not tell me. Years later, I learned it was because Howard stood up to Grandpa when he either did or was about to hit Grandma. This confirmed my dad's memory of hearing Grandpa and Grandma arguing and Dad standing up to his father, saying, "You will not hit Mom."

This revelation was hard for me to wrap my head around. It is difficult for me to imagine the silly, playful Grandpa laying hands on Grandma. However, it is not hard to imagine that someone who endured the traumas he did wouldn't have them come out somehow.

Grandpa did have a temper. Luckily it mellowed with age and grandkids. For me, it also explains some of Grandma's stances against arguing. She always said arguing is just not worth the time, and maybe that was her way of calming him and avoiding confrontation.

Witnessing domestic violence makes a child more likely to perpetuate it. I am blessed that this family trait was not passed down.

My father tells the story that on their wedding day, my mother's parents pulled them aside. To my father, they said, "If she ever does anything that causes you to want to hit her, put her on a bus and send her home. We will pay the fare." To my mother, they said, "Don't you ever do anything that causes him to want to hit you."

I'm not sure if they said this because they saw hints of trouble amongst my paternal grandparents or just because of the prevalence of abuse that existed in that day. Regardless, the message stuck, and good for us, my mom never went home on the bus.

Chapter 9
Raising My Siblings

The Hallman Siblings

Upton, Eugene, Pearl, Esther, Thompkins, Roberta, Melvin, and close family friend Frank Wint

The Making of a Pearl

Anyone who does not provide for their relatives, and especially for their own household, has denied the faith and is worse than an unbeliever.

I Timothy 5:8 (NIV)

All four of my brothers served in the army. Each of them served a two-year term. I saw all of them off. Mama never went; she just couldn't take seeing her sons go away to war. Papa and I would go to Rockville to see them get on the bus and go off to service. Thompkins served in Guinea during World War II. My father's family claimed to have descended from there. None of my brothers ever talked about their experiences in the military. And we were too afraid to ask.

We were blessed that they all made it home alive and physically unharmed. But that doesn't mean it didn't affect them. It affected Upton the most. He was stationed in Korea just after the end of WWII. He was always quiet, but after returning from Korea, he seemed quieter still. He was diligent, always kept a job, and got his work done.

He was working at the Naval Medical Center sorting clothes for the soldiers coming home. When World War II ended, more and more of the White soldiers were coming back, and they needed jobs. The Medical Center told Upton that he would have to give up his job to one of these soldiers. Something about how they said it set him off, and he snapped. He started yelling and throwing things.

Mama got a call that he was in the hospital. They said he had a mental break. From then on, he was never quite right. He would talk to himself and rock back and forth. He stayed with Mama and Papa for a little while, but they couldn't control him. He would wander off, and we would find him sitting somewhere in the cold, rocking and talking to someone we couldn't see. We just couldn't talk any reason into him anymore.

With Mama and Papa both working, it was just too much for them to watch him, work their own jobs, and manage the little ones. They decided to put Upton in a mental hospital in Baltimore. He would stay there during the week and come home some weekends. It was hard to see him like that. When you looked in his eyes, there was nothing there. But sometimes, just sometimes, he would look at you

Raising My Siblings

and smile or say something, and you could tell that deep inside, Upton was still in there.

I had my own family now, but I always tried to look out for my siblings. Bertie was now in college to become a teacher. After high school, she went to the local college, and then she was able to start at Morgan State. This meant moving to Baltimore. There weren't any opportunities for her to get her master's degree here, so she had to go to New York. We always hoped she would come back to Maryland and start teaching here close to us, but God had other plans.

She got a job at Knoxville College, a small Black college in Tennessee. She started as a teacher's assistant, but she eventually went on to get her doctorate, became a professor, and ultimately was president of the school. When she was first starting out, I knew she didn't have much money, so I would send her care packages with cans of sardines or Vienna sausages and packets of cookies and crackers. Any little thing that could help her get by.

Once she started teaching, I would send her my free Fashion Frock dresses. She was taller than me, so I would take the hem out so it would fit. With studying all the time, she told us she didn't have much time to get something to eat or shop for new clothes. But I knew the real problem was money. She didn't have much, and there wasn't much that our family could give her. The school had given her a scholarship for tuition and a place to stay, but not much more than that. She later told me that those care packages were like manna from heaven.

Me, Mama, Papa, and Esther flew down to Tennessee for Bertie's graduation. This was the first time that any of us had flown. Papa loved it; he spent the whole flight staring out the window, just amazed at how high up we were. We stayed in a hotel and were all looking forward to sleeping in. But wouldn't you know, Papa was still up at 6:00 am asking us to get him breakfast. We could take him off the farm, but we couldn't take the farm routine out of him.

After high school, Melvin went to the Milwaukee School of Engineering. He was the first in our family to go to college; we couldn't believe he was going to be going so far away. Being away was hard for him too, and he ended up taking a break to do his military service. After his time in the army, he transferred to Howard University in Washington, DC, where he got his bachelor's degree in electrical engineering. He first took a job at the Johns Hopkins Applied Physics Laboratory and then spent thirty years at the US Navy Department.

The Making of a Pearl

Melvin always loved tinkering with things, taking them apart, and putting them back together. At one point, he gave us this nice radio for Christmas. Then he came back at spring break to say he needed it to take apart for school. I don't think he ever quite got the radio back to how it was supposed to be.

He married Sylvia, and they had two sons, David and Dwight. Melvin and Sylvia were never meant to be, and they ended up divorcing. After retiring from a career in engineering, he decided to follow his passion. He got a degree in social work and started counseling young people.

Eugene, or Gene as we called him, was more of a free spirit. He served two years in the army during the Korean War. While he never developed the schizophrenia that Upton did, the war affected him too. Mostly in the form of a temper, but he managed to keep himself out of trouble with the law. He worked for the school system for almost forty years. He never married and lived at the homeplace until we had to sell it, and they tore it down.

Esther—though she and I are twenty-one years apart in age—is the sibling I am closest to. She has been my daughter, sister, and best friend. When Peaches and Vernon were little, she used to babysit them. One day she decided she would make biscuits. Well, she hadn't quite perfected her baking skills yet. The rolls were so hard the boys used them for baseball practice. She's come a long way, though. After she retired, she started a catering business. The food was excellent, but her husband made most of the rolls.

She married and built a house on the land that Papa had given her, which was just up the street from Gerard's step-daughter Helen and her husband, Charles. I made her wedding dress for her; she was a beautiful bride. She and Henry had two daughters, Pam and Darlene. Everything on the outside seemed happy, but we later learned that things were not as good as they appeared. Somehow Gene got word that Henry was being abusive to Esther. He would not stand for his little sister to be disrespected, and he marched himself right up to Henry and punched him. They tussled outside of Mama's house until Papa went and broke it up.

Esther and Henry separated but then got back together. Eventually, they separated for good. Gerard had a friend, Curtis, from NIH, and they would play checkers together during the night shifts. He was a little rough around the edges but had a good heart. Gerard and a few friends worked on Curtis to smooth his edges and eventually introduced him to Esther. He made her so happy. They married in 1980 and have been happy together ever since. They started a travel club, went on many cruises, and started a catering business.

Reflections on Raising My Siblings

The war certainly left an impact on Grandma's brothers. Thompkins served in the Army and, after basic training was stationed on the USS Monticello in Papua New Guinea. Now one thing to note is that Grandma is notoriously bad at geography. She always thought it a remarkable coincidence that Thompkins was stationed in Papua New Guinea and that her father had some ancestral roots in Guinea.

She chuckled at the irony that Thompkins would be stationed where her ancestors were from. She never comprehended—after multiple attempts to explain the difference—that Papua New Guinea, off the coast of Australia, and Guinea, on the west coast of Africa, were on opposite sides of the world.

Thompkins worked as a clerk typist prior to joining the military. One day he was asked to deliver something to the White officers' headquarters. Those were entirely separate from the Black servicemen's area, and he ambitiously jumped on a bicycle for the first time in his life to deliver the message. While there, they discovered that he was skilled in dictation and typing, and from then on, he left his unit and traveled with the officers to Manilla, Philippines.

They had orders to go to Japan, but en route, the bombs were dropped on Hiroshima and Nagasaki ending the war and his time in the service. On his way home, he traveled through Tokyo, California, Salt Lake City, Chicago, and Baltimore before landing in Washington, DC, where he surprised Grandma on the streetcar on her way back to Rockville after work.

Mental illness in the Black community is rarely talked about, and my family is no different. When I was a child, I didn't understand why Uncle Upton was so quiet and had a tic of his mouth and a tremor in his hand. Later, in medical school, I would learn those were the tell-tale side effects of antipsychotic medications.

Uncle Upton lived in a mental health institution for most of his adult life. I don't know what his experience was there. I don't know if he thrived or was overly medicated and sedated. But I do know he was safe, clean, well-fed, and off the streets. His presence at family events was important, even if it was quiet. While his diagnosis may not have been talked about, he himself was not a secret to be hidden.

Many mental health institutions were cruel and inhumane, with residents suffering abuse. Over the past few decades, there has been a push to deinstitutionalize those with severe mental illness. The goal is to provide them with better support so that they can live independently in the community rather than locked up in an institution.

While the effort is laudable, the support needed to enable someone with severe mental illness to live independently has not materialized, at least not on a large scale. As a result, today, most of our mentally ill sit in prisons or on the streets homeless. While I do not advocate for a return to large-scale institutionalization, without putting more support in place for community-dwelling, we are condemning some of our most vulnerable to a fate no better than the institution we were supposed to be protecting them from.

While Uncle Upton's schizophrenia was hiding in plain sight, what is even more insidious is the depression and anxiety left undiscussed. My ears, finely tuned for eavesdropping, overheard Aunt Esther sharing that she had battled depression silently and alone. Grandma's grief was pushed down and buried somewhere deep inside of her.

We are proud people with no time to wallow in our feelings. Yet, that worldview does a disservice to us. Depression is more than just feeling down; it is an illness with physical manifestations. Like other chronic illnesses, such as hypertension and diabetes, it, too, is treatable. Depression is not a sign of weakness or lack of faith. I am proud to see the younger generation is starting to break down some of the stigma around therapy and medication for treatment.

Chapter 10
A Changing Community

Pleasant View, Hunting Hill, and McDonald Chapel, the three churches that merged to form Fairhaven United Methodist Church

The Making of a Pearl

> *[18]Forget the former things; do not dwell on the past.*
> *[19]See, I am doing a new thing! Now it springs up; do you not perceive it? I am making a way in the wilderness and streams in the wasteland.*
>
> *Isaiah 43:18-19 (NIV)*

School desegregation was a big thing for our community, but it was only the beginning of changes that were coming for Quince Orchard. For Peaches, I'm sure it took some adjusting, but many of the White students he went to school with he already knew from the neighborhood. And for Vernon, integrated schools were all he ever knew.

As they grew, I know they sometimes felt alone. They both were good students and often found themselves as the only Black person in their classes. We continued to be active at Pleasant View church. I taught Sunday school and played the piano. The boys went to youth fellowship and other activities. While the church remained the center of our community, the church and area around Quince Orchard were changing.

It was the 1960s, and it felt like the whole world was changing. People were marching for civil rights and desegregation. The pictures from down south were just horrifying—people getting attacked by dogs, sprayed by water hoses, and humiliated while just trying to have lunch. The assassination of President John F. Kennedy saddened us all, but the death of someone closer, just one month later, changed our world even more.

Snyder's Store was our community center. It was an old country store with penny candy and essentials like flour, sugar, and eggs. The owner, Donald Snyder, always had a collection of odds and ends—old antiques and other things you might need one day. The store seemed cluttered, but he always knew where everything was. When we were young, we would go and trade an egg for a piece of candy. Or sit out front and talk with friends while we drank a soda. There was a gas station; if you needed gas, Snyder would come out to the car and work the hand crank.

Donald Snyder was White, but he treated all of us the same as kids; Black and White, it didn't matter to him. He was pretty quiet and kept to himself. He wasn't married and didn't have any children of his own. He lived above the store with his brother and sister-in-law.

A Changing Community

Their mother was almost deaf. She would come to the store on Sunday mornings. They fashioned a speaker wire from the church across the street, McDonald Chapel, and into the store so she could hear the services.

Snyder owned a lot of land in the area, so it was always rumored that he was rich. If he was rich, you couldn't tell it by looking at him. His clothes were certainly nothing special, and the store was far from fancy. He always seemed to be in the same boat as the rest of us. But the rumors persisted, and one day a man from Bethesda acted on them.

One snowy day in December 1963, just before Christmas, a man came into the store and asked for cigarettes. When Snyder turned to get them, the man shot him in the head. Another man who was out getting gas came in shortly after, saw Snyder, and called the police. They later found the killer. He reportedly told his mother, "I didn't mean to kill him; I thought he was going for his gun."

The rumors of him being rich and having lots of money stashed somewhere were just rumors. Snyder was rich in land—owning several houses and many acres—but he only had enough cash on hand to run the store.

It seemed like that shot tore through our small community and changed it forever. We didn't feel as safe anymore. It wasn't strange to have a gun, especially for the farm, but we never used them on people. After Snyder was shot, his family sold the store and surrounding land, and a shopping center was put in. Around the same time, the National Bureau of Standards moved from Washington, DC, to Gaithersburg and brought with it many new people. New houses were being built everywhere, and it started to feel like our Quince Orchard community was disappearing.

More and more of the younger generation was growing up and leaving Quince Orchard for jobs in the city. Howard had moved to Washington, DC, and so had Thompkins, though he came back each week for Sunday service. Bertie was down south. The membership at Pleasant View was dwindling. The tithes and offerings of the members were not enough to support the needs of the church.

The church hosted chicken dinners almost every weekend to help raise money. They really were just pulling from themselves as the same people both prepared and purchased the dinners. Pleasant View wasn't the only church in Quince Orchard with a struggling membership. Hunting Hill and McDonald Chapel, both White

The Making of a Pearl

Methodist churches, had the same issues. Pleasant View sat between these two churches, which were less than two miles apart.

Sunday mornings at Pleasant View had changed from when I was little. The service was still lively, with good preaching and great singing. But the attendance was much smaller. I had passed my piano-playing duties down to my sister Esther. I was still teaching Sunday school and singing in the choir. The whole family was active; we poured ourselves into that little church to keep it going.

Sunday services at McDonald Chapel and Hunting Hill were almost identical to each other, though not nearly as lively as Pleasant View. Each congregation largely consisted of a single large White family and their close friends. Since the churches were so small and couldn't support themselves, it was suggested that they merge into one. And yet, despite their close proximity, their identical worship styles, and shrinking membership and funds, they initially resisted merging.

Talk of a merger started coming around when we got a new minister, Rev. Douglas Horton. Rev. Horton was White, but he had marched with Dr. King and asked to pastor our Pleasant View church. We welcomed him with open arms. His son was just precious, and Vernon often babysat him.

When Rev. Horton first started talking about Pleasant View merging with Hunting Hill and McDonald Chapel, my brothers Thompkins and Melvin were all for it. Gerard, on the other hand, was not. Gerard's grandfather, Gary Green, helped build Pleasant View church, and he didn't want to see it lost.

Gerard was head of the trustees, an usher, and the treasurer. He doubted whether he could hold similar prestigious roles if they merged with White congregations. That divide was happening in other families too. Some were in favor of the merger; others opposed it. The younger generation was almost entirely in favor. They had grown up in integrated schools and knew the kids of these churches well. Peaches was for the merger, and with his father against it, those created some tense days in our house.

It all came to a head on April 4, 1968. Pleasant View decided to have a dinner meeting to discuss the merger. We met in the old schoolhouse where many of us had gone to school as children. Rev. Horton invited a speaker to come from Washington, DC, to talk about the merger and what other churches had done. We were eating and waiting, but the speaker still had not arrived from Washington, DC.

A Changing Community

Time seemed to be dragging. Rev. Horton and Melvin went out to the car to listen to the radio and traffic report to see what might be holding him up. A little while later, they both came back in. Before they said anything, you could tell from their faces that something was terribly wrong. The room got quiet, and all eyes turned to look at them. Rev. Horton choked up as he said that Rev. Martin Luther King, Jr. had been shot and killed.

The room just broke down in screaming and crying. Rev. Horton took us all outside, and we gathered around the flagpole to pray. As he prayed, you could see the tears streaming down Rev. Horton's face just as much as all of us. It was obvious that Rev. King meant just as much to him, a White man, as he did to us.

Obviously, with that news, the meeting fell apart. We stopped discussing the merger, and we did not take a vote. The time after Rev. King died felt like moving through mud. Everyone's heart was heavy. Washington, DC, was on fire with people looting and rioting. I was worried about Howard, who was living downtown at the time. For some, Rev. King's death made them feel even more strongly that we should not merge with the other two churches. If Whites could kill Rev. King, what would they do to us?

We had so many questions. There were so many things we didn't know. Would we get any respect in this new church? Would they just expect us to be the janitors and the maids? We kept Pleasant View going for generations with our family buried in the graveyard. What would happen to all of that if we merged?

For others, King's death emboldened us and showed us that the merger was even more urgent now. What better way to fulfill Rev. King's dream than to come together with two White churches? After a few weeks, we came back together and took a secret vote. The vote came out in favor of the merger. I was worried about how we would be treated, but also excited about something new. My parents never said how they felt one way or the other, but they came along with us and never complained.

Gerard, however, was not pleased with the outcome. And he wasn't the only one. Several broke off and joined other churches like Poplar Grove and Jerusalem Baptist. But most of us decided to work together to build this new thing.

One Sunday in September, several of us from Pleasant View went together to McDonald Chapel. We sat in the back, and when the pastor asked if there were any visitors, we all stood up and said we wanted to transfer our membership.

The Making of a Pearl

Transferring our membership rather than merging allowed us to keep the Pleasant View property with the church and schoolhouse. And most importantly, we kept the graveyard where so much of our family is buried. Several of us became trustees of Pleasant View, stewards to keep it in existence. The site was and still is too precious to lose. Gerard became the chair of the Pleasant View trustees, but he did not join the new church that would be named Fairhaven.

The three churches started worshiping together in September 1968 when we from Pleasant View transferred our membership. Through fundraising, loans, and money from the conference, we finally broke ground on a new building, Fairhaven, in 1970. It sat on an old farm just behind where I grew up. The name Fairhaven refers to Paul's stopping at the port of Fair Havens (Acts 27:8-19) for repairs to his boat before continuing to Rome with the Good News of Jesus Christ. It was an appropriate name because the merger of these three churches was not always smooth sailing.

Rev. Horton, who had been instrumental in the merger, was replaced in July of 1969 by Rev. William Heslop. Several of the members of the White churches thought Rev. Horton was too pushy on the issue of the merger and complained to the bishop. But those of us from Pleasant View were disappointed that the man who had worked so hard to help the merger couldn't see it all the way through.

The youth groups and women's groups from the churches had already started meeting together even prior to the merger. And, of course, the children were already going to school together. Even though many of us knew each other, it still wasn't easy in the beginning. All three churches lost members because they did not want to merge.

Several in the new congregation, Black and White, took it upon themselves to help encourage folks to mix. An example was a White woman, Bunny Heller; if she saw that all the Blacks were sitting on the left, then she would sit on the left. My brother, Thompkins, would do the same with a group of all Whites. The merger worked because people made it work. It didn't happen all at once just because we were all sitting in the same space. We still must work at it today, more than fifty years later. But the love you feel when you're open to any culture and family is unmatched.

It had been over ten years now since Pleasant View merged with Fairhaven. The people merged and attended service in a new church, but the original building and schoolhouse were still standing. We rented out the church for another congregation, and their rent helped

A Changing Community

to maintain the site. One of the churches even put in a set of stairs outside the building to make it easier to get into the basement. But with new developments going up all around, we started to worry that the site would be lost.

Gerard continued to be the head of the trustees, just like he was when the church was operational. He would tend to the grounds and cut the grass every other week. He made sure the gravesite was kept up; our parents and grandparents were all buried there. Mine have headstones, but Gerard's do not, and we know there are more buried there than we have records for. Every Memorial Day, I go back to tend the graves and put flowers out for my family.

Around this time, the county was starting to preserve other historical landmarks, and we learned they were giving money to do so. This little schoolhouse, one of the first in the county to educate Black children, was too precious to lose. We decided to start having an event every May to bring back the former students of the school and church members to recognize and remember the site. We would have food and a program with singing and performers.

We opened up the schoolhouse and church for tours. Helen would lead the children in the wrapping of a maypole, but they never seemed to get it just right. Many people who used to go to the church or attend the school would come back, and many of the new people who had moved into the community would come too.

It was a great time for fellowship; it reminded me of when we used to have Camp Meetings. The children would be playing, and Gerard always yelled at them to stay out of the graveyard. Seems like every year, a snake would show up that the men would have to kill. We would have speakers come from the county government and NAACP. There were performers for the kids, gospel choirs, and dancers. It kept that sense of community connection that seemed to be slipping away as more houses and shops came into the area. It was a time for those who remembered what Quince Orchard used to be to share some of that with their children and grandchildren.

We formed a historical society to help preserve the Pleasant View church and schoolhouse. We raised money and petitioned the county government to have the site listed as one of the historic places in the county. When we learned of its acceptance into the historical record, we were so excited. This meant we had funding to restore the building that was starting to crumble. But it also meant this site could not be torn down and would remain there for our grandchildren and their children to remember.

We were active in other ways too. The little lane where Helen and Charles, and Esther and Gerry lived was just a dirt road off the main road. It was a bad road, and whenever it rained or snowed, it would become impassable. We petitioned the county to get it named as a road. Once this was done, it was officially a county-maintained road which meant that it would be paved and plowed when it snowed.

We had a great ribbon-cutting ceremony on the day when the new road was commissioned. Papa Bell, Howard's grandfather, who was 100 years old and living at the end of the road, cut the ribbon. Kisha's brownie troop carried the flags. We named the streets Fellowship Lane and Fellowship Way.

The neighborhood continued to grow and change, and they started building a new high school just across the street from our house on Quince Orchard. By now, Donald Snyder's store was long gone, and there was a shopping center with a grocery store and doctor's offices. A podiatrist went in, and I started going to him for my foot. There was a McDonald's and a Wendy's right there on the corner that we could walk to.

We started hearing rumors about the name for the high school. Potomac Valley High is what they wanted to call it. Potomac was a good ten miles from here, so it didn't make any sense to us why they would call it that.

All of us from the Quince Orchard community, Black and White, started meeting to protest the name. We met with county officials to voice our opinion and started a letter-writing campaign to name it Quince Orchard. And ultimately, it did work. I am so grateful for this because I believe that had it not gotten the name Quince Orchard then how would people ever know that the Quince Orchard area was a place worth remembering. On the flip side, though, they ended up renaming the area North Potomac.

Reflections on A Changing Community

Hunting Hill and McDonald Chapel were both extension churches of larger Methodist congregations in Gaithersburg that had been established in the Quince Orchard farming community in the 1800s. In 1844 the Methodist Episcopal Church (MEC) split over the issue of slavery. That rippled throughout the country, even to Gaithersburg, where two churches emerged—Epworth, which sided with the MEC north, and Grace, which sided with the MEC south. Epworth went on to found Hunting Hill, and Grace founded

A Changing Community

McDonald Chapel. While some African Americans further splintered and formed the African Methodist Episcopal denomination, many remained with the MEC North and were placed in their own conference called the Central Jurisdiction, which stretched from the East Coast to the Midwest.

So, here, in the small town of Quince Orchard, sat a northern White Methodist church, a southern White Methodist church, and an African American Methodist church, all within two miles of each other. All with shrinking populations. All losing members to the big city. All hosting chicken dinners and lady's teas to stay afloat.

The members of each of these churches were not strangers. They lived on the same streets. Now, post-segregation, their children went to school together. Their youth groups had already merged, sharing fellowship together on Sunday nights. So too, had their women's guilds, as they were already planning projects and events together. And yet, while they were integrated in so many ways, their Sunday mornings remained very separate.

The Methodist church started efforts to reunify in the 1940s. The northern and southern divisions came back together into one Methodist Episcopal Church. The MEC then merged with the Evangelical United Brethren in 1968 to form the United Methodist Church. In the late 1960s, the Baltimore-Washington Conference, the conference to which Hunting Hill and McDonald Chapel were a part, began discussing uniting with the Central Jurisdiction to which the African American churches belonged.

Hunting Hill and McDonald Chapel, though separate churches, already shared a minister, Rev. Douglas Horton. This was common for small Methodist churches at that time. Pleasant View's minister, who was Black, came from quite a distance to preach every Sunday, and he too had several churches in his charge, the term for all the churches served by one pastor. None of the churches were big enough to support having one dedicated pastor.

Rev. Horton spoke with the minister of Pleasant View and offered to add it to his charge. This would be easy for him as he was already in the area and ministering to the congregations of the other two churches.

Easy for him but quite an adjustment for Pleasant View, who had never before had a White minister. Rev. Horton had been inspired by the civil rights movement. He walked with Rev. Martin Luther King, Jr. in Selma across the Edmund Pettus Bridge in 1965. He was a strong proponent of the work the Methodist church was doing to integrate churches. Though he was welcomed by our family, I'm sure the greater community murmured discontent about his preaching style.

Church mergers are difficult and often don't work. Usually, the bigger church absorbs the smaller, and the customs and traditions of the smaller church disappear into those of the bigger. Merging racially disparate churches is even harder. The merger was a process that happened over time rather than a singular event.

They were thoughtfully intentional in everything from the leadership of organizations to the hymns sung to the communion vessels used. For example, initially, they had Black and White co-chairs for every organization to try to make it equal. But that had the opposite effect; the Whites would go to the White chair and the Blacks to the Black chair. Eventually, they decided that one year would have a Black president and a White vice-president, and the next year it would switch. That way, everyone always knew who was in charge.

It also helped when they went to events with other churches. Whoever the president was would represent Fairhaven at Black and White churches alike. Every group and committee was integrated—the choirs, the Sunday school teachers, the communion stewards, and the kitchen committee. Administration and leadership—the ones that directed the church business, the pastor/parish relations committee, the trustees, and the finance committee—were also integrated.

In the 1980s, several of the Black congregants got together to discuss the needs of the African American members of the church. From that, they formed a gospel choir and added to the pews the Songs of Zion hymnal that had more spirituals. They started hosting gospel concerts and invited choirs from other churches to sing. Fairhaven also saw its first Black minister, Rev. Martin McKenny. They have since had three more Black ministers, one Korean, and its first female pastor in 2013.

I was baptized at Fairhaven and attended services there until I was ten. It still feels like home to me. My best friends growing up were at church. We played together while our parents were at choir rehearsal, cheered from the sidelines of the church softball games, and stormed the playground after Sunday service. Black kids and White kids all played together. Miss Emma, Grandma's cousin, yelled at Black kids and White kids the same. None of us could escape her watchful eye and her scolding to stop acting up in church.

She ran the kitchen with an iron spatula for all events, and everyone obeyed her instructions.

While Fairhaven had a gospel choir and eventually got a Black minister, it did not feel like a traditional Black church. It certainly felt different than my mom's traditional Black Baptist church that we attended when we visited her family in Ohio.

Part of that was the difference between more spirited Baptists and subdued Methodists. But part of it was the difference between one being integrated and the other not. Don't misunderstand; I felt the holy spirit moving in both churches and would not say that one was more spiritual or faithful than another. But the expressions of that spirit were different.

My experience at Fairhaven continues to shape my expectations of what church should be. In 2015 we even welcomed our first gay family, two White dads with four Black children. Fairhaven is the perfect place for them, and I wish more churches would be as welcoming.

Chapter 11
From Peaches to Gerry

From Peaches to Gerry

Peaches and Gerard

Gerry and Rita's Wedding

The Making of a Pearl

When I was a child, I talked like a child, I thought like a child, I reasoned like a child. When I became a man, I put childish ways behind me.

Corinthians 14:25 (NIV)

While the church merger was happening in our community, change was also happening in our family. Peaches, now a senior in high school, decided he wanted to go away for college. He heard about Mount Union College from his counselor at school. Gerard and I had never heard of the place. Once he had his mind set that that was where he wanted to go, there was no changing it. It was all the way out in Ohio, and Gerard could not understand why Peaches would want to go that far for school. There were plenty of good schools in Maryland. Bertie had gone to Morgan State in Baltimore, and the University of Maryland was now accepting Black students.

In the spring of 1968, Gerard and Peaches took the bus to Alliance, Ohio, to visit the school. Gerard didn't like to travel, and that bus trip was a good reminder of why. They went up through the mountains, and the bus felt like it was swinging and would tip over. At one point, the suitcases fell off the rack overhead. But they arrived safely at the school and toured it.

Peaches fell in love with Mount Union. Gerard did think it was nice and felt better about him going. There was no stopping him now. Later that fall, we packed up the car and all drove out to drop him off. We took his belongings to his dorm and got him set up. We didn't see him again until winter break at Christmas time. We didn't have enough money to buy Peaches bus fare at Thanksgiving, so he stayed in Ohio with a friend.

Peaches seemed to settle into college just fine. And we settled into a new rhythm at home. It was quieter now with Howard living in DC and Vernon in junior high. I had more time and decided to go back to work to help pay tuition. I started working at National Geographic, which was right down the street from us, much closer than when I used to have to go to Washington, DC, or even Rockville to work. I worked in accounting, keeping track of the subscriptions and what was paid. I was always good with numbers, and I still do the adding for my Avon orders by hand.

I enjoyed being with the other ladies and enjoyed the extra money it gave us. With Peaches in college, every extra bit helped. His tuition was due every three months. Gerard covered all the household expenses, and I paid for the schooling. Going back to work also gave me a new market of ladies to start selling my Avon to. My manager was okay with me selling, but I couldn't advertise it. So, I would get to work early and go around and place the Avon books under the ladies' stack of work and bring their packages back in brown paper bags.

During the fall of 1969, his second year, Peaches brought a group of students from Mount Union down to march on Washington, DC, to protest the Vietnam War. They had borrowed a bus that one of them drove. We put them up in the parish house at Pleasant View and they all slept on the floor. We made them meals and enjoyed their company. Among them was Bill Outlaw, Peaches' roommate, whom we met when we picked him up. All of his friends were calling him by his new name, Gerry.

Peaches had been trying to get us to call him Gerry since he came home from school after his first semester. It could never quite stick. He wasn't Gerry; he was just our Peaches. But, seeing him in this way, a leader among his friends organizing this trip, made us look at him differently. Even Gerard looked at him with a new sense of pride, not that he would ever tell him that. His friends called him Gerry, and we started calling him that too.

Gerry finished school at Mount Union. Gerard, Vernon, and I all drove out for the graduation in the spring of 1972. We saw many of the friends he had brought down for the Vietnam War protest several years before. We also finally got to meet Rita's parents. It was good to see Rita again.

We first met Rita when she and Gerry surprised us with a trip home. Gerard and I had just sat down to have supper, and here comes this knock on the door. The person on the other side didn't wait for us to answer it, the door just opened, and people started coming into the house. Here it is; Gerry, and right behind him, Bill, his college roommate. Then comes a woman who we assume to be Rita. She was my same complexion, with a big afro and cat eyeglasses. Gerry and Bill had afros, too; seemed like all the young folk did.

The house was a mess. Gerard was working on an addition off the dining room, and the opening was covered with plastic. I just had on my house coat.

Gerry says, "I have someone I want you all to meet. This is Rita, who I've been telling you about." They were obviously in love; he was hanging all over her.

The Making of a Pearl

I said, "Hi Bill; hi Rita. I wish Gerry had let us know you were coming so we could have prepared a little bit. Sorry, the house is a mess. Would you like something to eat? We are just having leftovers. And what are you all doing here?"

Gerry launched into a story about how they had gone to pick up Bill's bed and were stopping by on the way back to Mount Union. That didn't make any sense because I knew Bill lived all the way in North Carolina, but Gerry said somehow it was on the way. I guess they were just taking a road trip like kids do.

Gerard seemed to like Rita right away. After they left, he kept saying how nice and polite she was. That she seemed like she would be good for Gerry to help him keep his head down to earth since he always had so many crazy ideas. And he liked her much better than the White girl, Sharon, that Gerry seemed so infatuated with his freshman year.

Gerry had started talking to this girl, Sharon, when he was first at Mount Union. We didn't even know much about her. He had mentioned her casually over the phone but never made it sound like it was anything serious. He spent Thanksgiving weekend with his friend Kim Smith, a guy he knew from campus.

While he was away, we got a call from Sharon's parents; her father was a minister in Cleveland. Apparently, they weren't too happy that our Black son was hanging around with their White daughter. This was so typical of Gerry. He was always trying to break the mold and go outside of what was expected. If you told him to do one thing, he would do the opposite. He needed to figure things out for himself, try and fail on his own. You couldn't tell him what to do.

Gerard called him once he got back to campus and chewed him out. I could hear him on the phone. I don't know if Gerry got a word in at all. "Why are this girl's parents calling me telling me to tell you to stay away from their daughter? Why are you messing around with this girl? Don't you watch the news? Do you know what they could do to you? Don't let me hear any more about you dating that girl. You don't even know her; you've only been at the school a few months. And your grades better be good. We sent you all the way to Ohio to get your education, not for you to be messing around with White girls."

I got on the phone and tried to calm him down. I just said, "Peaches, maybe she isn't the right one for you. If it's real love, and you take a break from each other for a while, then it will still last. Just don't see each other for a while. You need to focus on your studies so you can end the semester well."

He was upset. Her parents had also called their dorm mothers, who also told both Gerry and Sharon they were not to see each other. During Christmas break, Gerry got a call from Sharon. The phone was in the middle of the house, so we all heard it.

She called to say that she wasn't coming back to school the next semester because her parents were pulling her out. Her dad then gets on the phone and tries to say that Gerry wasn't why he was pulling her; rather, it was because her grades were poor, and she wasn't focusing like she needed to. She was going to go to school closer to home with fewer distractions.

Then her mother gets on the phone and tells Gerry that it was definitely because of him that they were withdrawing her and he should stay away. What a crazy family! He was heartbroken after that and spent the rest of the break sulking in his room.

Needless to say, we were very excited to have Rita come into the picture. Gerry and Rita had been together for a couple of years when he graduated. She was a year behind him in school and from Ohio. For the last couple of years, he spent Thanksgiving with her family since it was too expensive for him to come home. By the time he graduated in 1972, he had already proposed, and they planned to marry the following summer after she graduated. After graduation, Gerry came home, stayed with us, and worked during the summer. Then he moved to Boston to start a master's program at Boston College.

Gerry and Rita married on August 11, 1973, at her home church in Columbus, Ohio. Gerard, Vernon, Howard, and I all went out a few days early, but the rest of the family and friends rented a bus and drove up from Quince Orchard. It was a beautiful day! Rita was just lovely, and her family was warm and kind. They just welcomed us in like family. We would continue to get together with her parents, Earl and Evelyn, for years to come. Howard was the best man, and Vernon was one of the groomsmen. Bill, Gerry's best friend from college, played the organ.

Bill graduated a year before Gerry, moved to Maryland, and started teaching in the county schools. He was originally from North Carolina, and we became his family away from home. He even started a youth singing group called the Black Experience with Vernon, Esther's daughters Pam and Darlene, Helen's twins Sherry and

The Making of a Pearl

Cherry, and several of the other neighborhood kids. They would go around and sing at different events.

After Gerry and Rita's wedding reception was over, we changed clothes and got right back on the road. Sunday was the family reunion. Mama was hosting as usual. She had been preparing food all week, but losing Saturday to the wedding meant we needed to be up extra early on Sunday to get everything ready.

It might seem crazy to have the reunion and a wedding in different states on the same weekend, but not to us. While most of the people from our family that came to the wedding also went to the reunion, not everybody at the reunion came to the wedding. And the reunion was just as grand as ever. Mama made just about all the food, and my mother's brother, Thompkins, brought ice cream from Washington, DC.

After the wedding, Rita moved to Boston to be with Gerry. We would visit them there in the summer, and they would come home for the holidays. A couple years later, Gerry graduated from his master's program. Gerard and I took the bus up. Gerry surprised us with plane tickets to go back home. I had been on a plane once before to go to Bertie's graduation, but this was Gerard's first time. And he was not excited to try it.

He was so upset. He didn't say anything at first, but after they dropped us off at the airport, then he started. "Why would he get us these? The bus is a perfectly fine way to get back. They don't have enough money to buy us this; they should have saved it to get something more useful."

"Gerard," I said, "Gerry just wants to do something nice, and look how much sooner we will get home. It will only take one hour instead of eight."

He didn't say anything, just kept sulking. When we got on the plane, I thought it was so peaceful to be up in the air, sailing through the clouds. I looked over at Gerard. His knuckles were white as he gripped the armrest and stared straight ahead.

"Don't you want to look out the window and see the clouds?" I asked. He barely uttered a no and kept looking the other way. When we landed, I finally heard him let out a sigh of relief.

Gerard always liked both feet solidly on the ground. No planes, ships, or even elevators. He liked to be in control of where he was going and how he got there. I, on the other hand, enjoyed exploring new places and went on bus trips and train rides, cruise ships, and even traveled to the Holy Lands.

From Peaches to Gerry

I found it exciting to learn about new places and meet different people. He took comfort in the routine—in being in his own space, in the predictability of it. Growing up, his life was anything but predictable; with both of his parents dead and him being kicked out and on his own before the age of ten, his luxury was to be safe in a house he built with the assurance that he knew what was coming next.

After Gerry graduated from Boston College, he and Rita decided that they were going to move back to Quince Orchard and build a house. My father had given me and my siblings each an acre of land off of Quince Orchard Rd. Gerard also bought several acres of land in the same area.

He had one lot that he used for his farm and the other two lots he planned to give to Gerry and Vernon. He didn't feel like he needed to give Howard any land since Howard wasn't his son. So, I gave Howard a portion of my lot. Howard and Gerry's land plots were right next to each other, and when Gerry decided to build on his, Howard said that he would do the same. There were only a couple of other houses on the street. Esther lived there, along with Anna Talley and Papa Bell—Big Howard's sister and father.

Gerry found a modular home company to build his house. Howard was going to do the same but then didn't like the deal. He ended up never building on his lot. They had to clear the trees, dig a well, and put in a septic tank. In the summer of 1977, while Gerry and Rita were waiting for the house to be finished, they lived with us. By this time, Gerard had added an addition to our house with a spare bedroom and bathroom downstairs, as well as another family room. They moved into that space. It was so small for all of their stuff. They could just about touch everything while sitting on their bed.

The new house was supposed to be ready in the summer of 1978. But it wasn't. Problems with the water and the permits caused delays. The house was finished, but they couldn't get an occupancy permit to move in. They had a baby on the way, and that made them even more anxious to have the house completed.

Kisha, their first child, arrived in September 1978. Rita was so disappointed to be coming back to our little house and not moving into their new house. They had to put the bassinet in the hallway because there was no space in their room. They may have been disappointed, but Gerard and I weren't. We enjoyed having a baby around. Kisha had Gerard wrapped around her little finger. Gerard was scared to hold her, for fear he'd break her, and preferred to put her on a big blue pillow on his lap.

Reflections on From Peaches to Gerry

In order to fully appreciate Quince Orchard, one has to leave it. My grandmother didn't really know how different Quince Orchard was until she and Big Howard moved to Washington, DC. The same was true of my father when he left for college. The love, support, and sense of belonging that was developed growing up in Quince Orchard prepared them for trials and tribulations that would come later in life. Much like a pearl that can't achieve its full beauty until it is extracted from the mollusk, Dad needed to leave his protective bubble and experience the world.

Experience a new world he did. In college, he heard the word nigger directed at him for the first time. Had his first interracial dating experience. He heard world views very different from his own. It spurred him to activism, organizing a group to protest the Vietnam War. It tested and ultimately strengthened his faith.

Throughout the Bible are several instances where God changes someone's name—Abram and Sarai to Abraham and Sara, Jacob to Israel, and Simon to Peter. All are instances when God is calling someone to something greater. College was the beginning of Dad's calling that would lead him to become a minister. And it was the time of his own name change, leaving his childhood moniker, Peaches, behind to take on the cloak of adulthood in Gerry.

When I was in residency, an attending joked that teenagers lose their minds around age eighteen, so their parents won't feel bad about kicking them out. Dad was determined to leave before being kicked out, but he certainly had his disagreements with Grandpa. Much of that centered around the church merger, which Dad favored and Grandpa did not.

While Dad was around to advocate for the transition, he was away at Mount Union in September of 1968 when it actually occurred. He was away for college and graduate school for the next ten years and missed much of the growing pains that Fairhaven endured in its merger.

When my parents moved back to Quince Orchard, they were actively involved and helped to push Fairhaven to do more to consider the needs of the Black congregants—a throwback to their college activism. They were founding members of the gospel choir and were involved in a myriad of activities. About ten years after their joining, we left Fairhaven when Dad was ordained as a Methodist minister and appointed to his first church.

His role at Fairhaven has been that of an external force, nudging them closer to the ideal. Only in leaving Fairhaven did he gain the perspective and skills needed to help push it to live up to its potential.

Chapter 12
Our Changing Family

Curtis and Esther's cruise club to Jamaica

Pearl and Gerard

The Making of a Pearl

Give, and it will be given to you. Good measure, pressed down, shaken together, running over, will be put into your lap. For with the measure you give will be the measure you get back.

Luke 6:38 (NIV)

Mama's health started going downhill in the late 1970s. Eventually, she got so sick that we couldn't care for her at home, and she went to live at Asbury, a nursing home, in August of 1981. She had poor circulation in both her legs, and they had to cut them off at the knee. That was so hard for me to accept. It seemed like she lost a lot of her will to live once she lost her legs, even though she was already pretty much confined to the wheelchair.

One day a nurse said to me, "Pearl, I want you to go downstairs and talk to this lady."

I went to see her. She was so jolly, always laughing and friendly. We started talking, and I told her about how my mother had lost her legs. When I came in the next week to chat with the woman I'd met the week before, I was astonished to see her fake legs were detached and sitting over by the radio. I had no idea that she didn't have any legs, just like Mama. When I saw them there, I just cried. After that, we became great friends, and I felt like I could talk to her like I did my mother.

When I would visit Mama, I would also stop in to see other patients on her floor. I would help feed them or read a story. One day the head nurse said to me. "Pearl, I want you to go down to the first floor and wait on those people during lunch hour." I did, and when I returned, she said, "Your mother can feed herself, but she was thinking if you were going to feed anyone, why not be her?"

After that, whenever I was at Asbury during lunchtime, I would go down to the first floor and feed somebody else. I could give Mama ice and things like that, but when lunchtime came, I would always go down to the first floor. It gave her the tiniest sense of independence. Mama lived at Asbury until she passed in April of 1982.

After Mama died, Esther said we needed to do something fun, like take a vacation. She suggested we should go on a cruise. I didn't know what she was talking about with a cruise. Gerard and I had never taken a big vacation. We would go to Atlantic City, but never anywhere far. Gerard did not like planes or boats, so a cruise for him was out of the question. I tried to get him to come along, but he said, "Can't Bertie be your roommate?" And she was.

The cruises were just amazing. Esther would organize it, and we would go every other year. We would pay a little bit each month to make it manageable. I remember it just being so amazing. I never went to the dances, but I loved the shows and workshops like how to fold napkins. Such fancy dinners, food I could never get back in Quince Orchard. I always took my time eating and savored every bite. We got to visit new places like the Caribbean and Alaska. Relaxing and sitting out by the pool was just such a luxury.

It also made me realize how poor we were growing up. We had everything we needed and not a stitch extra. We grew our own food and made our own clothes. I didn't even know what a restaurant was until I started courting Howard. We didn't have any in Quince Orchard, and even if we did, how would we afford to take our family of ten out to eat?

And a vacation? Ha, that was something rich people did. Once Gerard and I had children, we would go for day trips to the beach or take a bus ride to the fair. But the idea of taking a whole week off, traveling to another country by plane and ship, and letting other people wait on you, well, that was just beyond my imagination. I still wouldn't call us anywhere close to rich, but at least there was a little extra money in our pocket to do something nice once in a while.

The family was growing and changing. Gerry and Rita had their second baby, Jason, in 1981. Once Kisha started school, Rita went back to work part-time, and I started keeping the children during the day. They would come to our house in the morning to catch the bus and get dropped off there in the afternoon. While Kisha was in school, Jason would be with me. He would go with me to Asbury and help deliver ice or run errands.

Once a week after school, they would help me do Avon. One week I would give them the Avon books, and they would run through the neighborhood and leave them on people's doors. The next week we would go back and deliver the packages. They were such good helpers.

Howard's boys, Kevin and Tim, were getting bigger too. Howard was living in Bowie, but the boys lived with their mother in Gaithersburg, so we got to see them some. Rita would tutor them in math when they were in middle school. With more children around, the holidays became even more special.

The Making of a Pearl

Because Kevin and Tim were with their mother, they didn't join us for the holidays. I started having an early Christmas that they could come to. In early December, I would fix a big dinner of country ham, turkey, and greens, and I always had to make my two special dishes, stewed tomatoes and sauerkraut. We started a tradition of giving out money for the family to use to buy Christmas gifts.

We gave the adults cash, but for the children, we gave them banks filled with quarters. The banks were made out of a coconut shell carved to look like monkeys. I had picked them up on one of my cruise adventures to the Caribbean. Each year the kids would break open the banks, pour out their quarters, and then sit there stacking the quarters into fours and making rows. Some were neater at this than others. Gerard and I both would just smile to see the family together and so happy. It made us feel so good to be able to give them a little something to buy gifts with.

In 1983, Gerry announced that he was accepting the call to ministry and would be going back to school for seminary. Gerard did not like this idea at all. All of the ministers he had seen growing up were poor and dependent on their congregation for everything. How was Gerry going to raise a family on a minister's salary? They had two kids now, Kisha and Jason, and a third, Maya, would arrive in 1987. But this wasn't the first time Gerard and Gerry disagreed, and just like in previous times, Gerry went on and did what he felt called to do. I tried to reassure Gerard by saying, "He will be okay. God is looking after them now." But he would just shake his head.

Gerry finished seminary in the spring of 1987, and Maya was born in November of that same year. He was doing a pastoral internship in Washington, DC. In 1988 he got his own church, Metropolitan UMC, about an hour away from us. I was excited for him; I knew this was what he wanted for some time. Gerard was worried, now they would be further away, and Gerry would have to rely on his congregation.

It was far, but not that far. We started having lunch every Wednesday. Rita would come back, and she, Esther, and I would go out to lunch. Each week we would alternate who paid, and whoever paid got to pick the place and say grace. If the kids were home from school or Bertie was in town, then they would come along with us.

It was 1988, and Esther was going to be forty-nine. Curtis wanted to have a surprise party for her. He said he didn't want to do it when she turned fifty because then she would be expecting it. The plan was for the party to be at the big Catholic church in Rockville. We had told her that we were going to a program at the church that Saturday afternoon, which was an excuse to get her to dress up. I was so excited about celebrating her and told everyone about this party that we were planning.

The night before the party, Esther and Curtis and Gerry and Rita and the kids were all over to our house. Esther said that she wasn't feeling well and that she wasn't sure if she would be able to make it to the program the next day. I told her, "Oh, just get some good sleep tonight. I'm sure you will be fine."

The kids were off playing, and Gerard seemed to have some extra energy that evening. He always perked up when the kids were around. It was a warm evening, and he and Jason decided to go for a walk outside. When they got back, Gerard was chuckling to himself, and Jason wore a big grin. Whatever secret they shared between them had them both acting silly.

The next day, Esther and Curtis picked up Gerard and me and drove us to the church. There were a lot of cars in the parking lot, and I was happy to see so many people had come out to celebrate Esther. As we were walking in, I saw Bill Outlaw sneaking in the back door. I waved at him trying to tell him to hurry to get inside.

When we walk in, everyone jumps out and yells surprise! I yelled surprise, too, because I thought we were surprising Esther. But they were actually surprising me for my seventieth birthday. Our birthdays are just three days apart. It was friends and family from all over. Even Bertie came up from Tennessee. The family had been planning this for months, secretly meeting at Gerry and Rita's house.

My siblings performed *This is Your Life* and told stories from us growing up. They had collected donations for me and attached the money to a big toy ship on wheels with a sign saying your ship has finally come in. I've always wanted to ride in a gray limousine with a White driver. Well, Sam Adams from church was a limousine driver, and they arranged for him to drive Gerard and me around after the party and then take us home. It was so nice to see all the family together. I've never been very comfortable being the center of attention; I'm used to being the one helping to plan things.

Jason and Gerard's late-night stroll was Jason telling him about the party. Jason knew Gerard's health was declining and didn't want to shock him with the surprise; at least, that is what he said. To this day, Jason still gets teased about not being able to keep a secret.

Around this time, Gerard truly started having trouble with his health. His body was wearing down. At first, he didn't want to even admit that he was having any trouble, but I could tell he was moving slower. Then it hit. One day he couldn't move his arm and couldn't speak. We went to the hospital and learned that he had had a stroke. His blood pressure was high, and he had to start medication for that. He started therapy for his hand to get his function back. What seemed to work the best was using a weaving loom and having to thread the loops through each other. He made so many potholders.

He did get most function back, but his hand was still weak. Sometimes it would freeze up when he would try to lift a glass. One time the whole family was out at a restaurant, and he spilled his glass of water on the table. He was so sad about it. He felt like a child being clumsy. He was frustrated that the physical strength that he had depended on for his entire life was failing him. When Gerry's family moved, it seemed like it took some of the life out of him. Not being able to see the grandkids every day lowered his spirits.

He got better, and then he had another stroke and got worse again. It affected a similar area of his brain, and much of the progress he made went away. He had to start all over again by working his hands and his speech. But he did it. This time it wasn't as severe as the first. But what it seemed to take away even more was his spirit. Then we found out that he had leukemia, and there wasn't really any treatment to cure it; we just had to monitor it.

He was getting weaker. It was harder for him to go up and down the steps, so he stayed in the bedroom downstairs. He was in so much pain, and often you would hear him singing, "Precious Lord, Take Me Home." When we could still get around, we would try to get out each day and go somewhere for a drive or out to eat.

He started having trouble with his bowels and bladder. One time we were out to eat, and he went to the bathroom. He was in there for a long time, so I went to check. I stood at the door and called into the men's room. At first, I didn't hear anything, but then I heard him moaning and crying. I went in and found him in the stall. He had messed in his pants. I told him to hang on; I was coming. Luckily there was a change of clothes in the car. I went out and got that and then went on into the men's room to help him get cleaned up.

We didn't finish our lunch, just went on back home. He cried the whole way home, "I feel just like a baby needing a diaper."

I tried to comfort him, but he wouldn't hear it. We got home and got him in the house, and cleaned up even more. Around this time, Vernon moved back home to help out. He was a nurse and had started working at Asbury in the evenings. He was such a help to Gerard; he would help him with bathing and dressing.

We still would try to go out when we could. Gerard especially liked going to Dee Dee's Diner, Denny's, Big Boys, or even just getting an apple pie from McDonald's. Everyone knew him by name and was excited to see us coming. I tried to keep my regular routines as much as I could. I kept on selling Avon and volunteering at Asbury. Esther and Rita kept coming for our Wednesday lunch bunch. Gerard never wanted to go out with us even before he got sick, "too much lady talk," he said.

Eventually, he got so sick, and there was nothing they could do, so the doctors recommended that he start hospice. I wasn't really sure what that was, but someone would come to the house and help care for him. A volunteer would come to sit with him once a week for two hours to give me a break. They told me to be ready to leave the house when the volunteer arrived. When the volunteer would get there, guess where I went, Asbury, of course.

Some would say, you spend all day every day taking care of Gerard, and when you get a break, you go help take care of other people? But that was my life, you know. And Gerard loved it when the nurses came. I'd come in, and the nurse would just be rubbing his feet, and he would just be grinning. That time was a blessing for both of us.

I still kept cruising with Esther and Bertie. Gerard wasn't happy about that. He was worried that he would die while I was away. But I had faith that wouldn't happen. I felt in my spirit he still had some time left. And I knew that he would be fine with Vernon there to watch and the nurses coming in. I also needed some time to myself to prepare for what I knew was coming eventually. The cruise was nice, as they always are, and it was the relaxation that I needed. Just to sit out in the sun felt like a gift from God. But my mind was back home, praying for him and the boys taking care of him the entire time.

On a Wednesday in mid-September 1991, Gerry came over. He took Gerard in the wheelchair and wheeled him all throughout the neighborhood—up and down Quince Orchard Road and Fellowship Lane. When they returned, he sat on the couch for a bit and then went back to his hospital bed in the front room. Gerry was sitting with him as his breathing slowed. He called me over, and I kissed Gerard on the forehead.

The stopping of breath was almost imperceptible. He would breathe in softly, and you almost couldn't even hear him breathe out.

The Making of a Pearl

Then a sigh. Then you would wait for the next breath in. And then there wasn't one. Gerry prayed as we held hands around him. He prayed for Gerard, for his spirit to finally be at rest. No more pain. He prayed for me, to give me strength. He prayed for Vernon and the hospice nurses who had tended to him in those final days.

The funeral was a few days later; it felt like such a whirlwind. Family was all around. Vernon sang a solo, "Give Me My Flowers." Gerry gave remarks from the family. I was strong for everyone. I didn't cry. I don't cry easily. That September 29th would have been our 43rd wedding anniversary. That day was the hardest. Gerry came over, and we went to lunch.

Reflections on Our Changing Family

Asbury Methodist Village is a community for senior citizens that offers everything from villas and apartments for downsizing after retirement all the way through skilled nursing, rehab, and hospice. Asbury helped my great-grandmother when she was nearing the end of her life, but it continued to help my grandmother for decades after that. She continued to volunteer there until she had trouble walking.

Even after she stopped driving at the age of ninety-two, Grandma would have people drive her to Asbury so she could continue to volunteer and deliver Avon. Volunteering mostly consisted of visiting with people, reading them a devotional from the Upper Room, and sharing a story or memory. She gave people more than just ice or a trip to the common area. She gave them a sense of value and let them know that they were not forgotten. It was how she spread her love and received so much love at the same time. She spread connection and created community.

She built wonderful relationships with the staff as well. She became their Avon lady because she wouldn't miss an opportunity to sell. When Grandpa was sick and in hospice at home, Asbury and Avon became her escape. They were the protective shell protecting Pearl.

Later, when she fell ill due to an infection in the same foot that troubled her many years before, it was Asbury where she went for rehab. And when they were threatening to cut off her foot, much like the doctors recommended almost ninety years prior, the strength and faith she pulled on from being at Asbury led her to do the hard work to prove the doctors wrong yet again.

The staff she had interacted with for so many years were now proud to be taking care of the Avon lady. She was determined not to follow the same path as her mother. Not to have her foot cut off and not to spend her last days there.

Asbury and Avon, service and selling, were her mainstays and highlighted how she thrived on connections with people.

Considering the illness I had watched as a child with Grandpa getting sick and dying, you might assume that was my push to a medical career. However, my desire to become a doctor came four to five years earlier for no specific reason other than it seemed like a good thing to do. I continued to explore and confirm. If Grandpa's illness has influenced my career in any way, it was to highlight the benefits of hospice. Watching someone die is not an easy thing to do. Hearing them cry out in pain is difficult to hear.

When we would visit, he would sometimes be too ill to come out and sit with us. He would stay in his room, and we would hear him crying out, praying to God, and singing. And slowly, but eventually, my prayers changed from requesting healing to requesting comfort. I didn't know then what hospice was or that he received hospice care. All I knew was that people came to the house to help care for Grandpa and give my grandmother a break.

Hospice is care for terminally ill patients that focuses on quality of life, reducing pain and suffering, and addressing emotional and spiritual wellbeing. It also provides support to the family with the transition.

Hospice allowed us to keep Grandpa at home. I only have one memory of visiting my grandfather in a hospital, the Easter following a stroke he had on Good Friday. But I do remember him being at home, in his hospital bed, sometimes crying in pain, but as children, we could be with him. Hospitals are scary sterile places where children are not welcome. We were not shielded from his pain, but I also like to think that our presence gave him some strength.

Hospice is often not well received in the Black community. It is viewed with an eye of distrust. On average, Black patients see an increase in the intensity of healthcare services at the end of life. In a way, it may be an attempt to make up for lost time and care that wasn't received earlier in life.

Many Blacks falsely believe that by offering hospice, doctors are giving up on patients and not offering Black patients the same aggressive treatments they may offer to Whites. With the history of racism in this country—extending even into healthcare—I understand how that sentiment has taken root.

While nearly half of all White patients die under hospice care, less than a third of Blacks take advantage of this service. Hospice is often misrepresented as giving up on someone and hastening death. However, several studies have shown that terminally ill patients in hospice care live, on average, a month longer than those who did not receive hospice care. And those days in hospice tend to be more fulfilling days with less pain and suffering.

For our family, hospice offered a way to surround Grandpa with love, eased his pain, supported Grandma, and helped us all honor the man that we loved in his final days.

Chapter 13
Moving Forward

Pearl, Gerry, Maya, Kisha, Rita, and Jason at the Grand Canyon

The Making of a Pearl

"For I know the plans I have for you," declares the Lord, "plans to prosper you and not to harm you, plans to give you hope and a future."

Jeremiah 29:11 (NIV)

1991 was a hard year. A few months after Gerard died, on December 28, we learned that my brother Upton died at the age of sixty-nine. He was still living at the mental health facility. Esther did most of the work in planning his funeral and burial. It was hard losing him, but at the same time, it felt like we had lost the real Upton many years ago.

I slowly started putting the pieces of me back together. We cleaned out Gerard's room. They took out the hospital bed. The house stopped smelling like a hospital and started smelling like a house again. I kept up my Avon and kept going to Asbury. Esther and Rita, and I kept going to lunch. Everyone would ask me, "Ms. Pearl, are you okay?"

And I would say, "Oh yes. God is with me. I'm okay." And I was okay.

I had learned many years before not to grieve the loss of my husbands. That doesn't mean I didn't miss Gerard; I did. I missed his presence, his smile and laugh, his grumpiness. But when someone is sick for so long, when they spend so much time in pain, when they start to lose their dignity, and when they spend every night crying out for God to take them home, then you start to welcome death. I knew that Gerard was ready. He had lived a good life, a meaningful life. It gave me comfort to know that now he was with God and not suffering anymore.

Early in 1992, Gerry found out that he would be moving to a new church, Epworth United Methodist Church. It was right here in Gaithersburg, and they would be moving back to their old house just up the street from us. I was so excited about them moving back. I wished Gerard was still around to see it. Kisha was now starting high school, Jason in middle school, and Maya would be starting kindergarten.

They were within walking distance of the high school, and my house was on the way. Kisha decided that she would stop at my house for breakfast before school. She would come every morning, and we would read the *Upper Room* devotional and have breakfast together. I would share my stories with her.

Jason was a freshman when she was a senior, and I thought he would start coming to join us for breakfast. But boys don't have time for their grandmothers. So, it was just Kisha and me for those four years. I was so happy for her when she got into Duke because I knew she really wanted to go there. I didn't really know anything about the school, but anytime I would tell someone where she was going, they would say, "Oh, that is a good school." Gerard would have been so proud.

Although Jason didn't come to join me for breakfast, he did take me to the senior prom. The first year the school opened, there was no senior class, so instead of a senior prom for students, they had a senior citizens prom. Every year I would see the signs for it, and I had been waiting to go. Kisha was never into dances and those kinds of things, but Jason was. I got all dressed up, he brought me a corsage, and off we went. He would dance with me, but he would also take some of the other ladies out and spin them around in their wheelchairs. It was a great time; we went all four years that he was in high school.

Gerry was working really hard at his new church, Epworth. Rita was the Director of Education and did all the Sunday school and youth programs. He started off as the associate pastor and then became the senior pastor. Epworth was a predominantly White congregation. In many ways, it felt like coming full circle from the merger of Pleasant View with the two White congregations, Hunting Hill and McDonald Chapel, to form Fairhaven.

He was also still working full-time as a pupil personnel worker for the Howard County Public Schools. Then he started a doctoral program at Loyola in Baltimore. He would be up and down the road every day. He didn't let one thing suffer. As your kids get older, you don't stop worrying about them; you just worry about different things. I would constantly pray for him, for his safety driving, and just to have the strength to do it all.

In 1994 Gerry and Rita invited me to join them and the kids on a road trip to the Grand Canyon. I couldn't pass up a trip out west. We packed up their minivan and headed out. On the way, we stopped through Knoxville, Tennessee, and visited Bertie. There was a lot of driving. Kansas seemed to stretch on as one flat field for an entire day. Once we got to the Grand Canyon, it was just amazing. It looked so different from anything I had ever seen before. All of the rocks and

The Making of a Pearl

boulders looked like they had been carved by hand. God's creation is just beautiful.

When Gerry was still at Metropolitan, we would visit his church every now and then, and my siblings would come too for some of the special services. Melvin came to one of them and met one of Gerry's members, Evon. She seemed just right for him. Melvin and Evon dated and later married, and Gerry did the ceremony at Metropolitan. They bought a big house together and hosted Thanksgiving every year.

In January 1997, Evon called Esther frantic, saying she couldn't wake Melvin up. She had already called 911, and the paramedics came and pronounced him dead. It was shocking to us as he was the healthiest among us and only sixty-four. He was a Seventh-day Adventist and had maintained a strict vegetarian lifestyle for many years. We later found out that he had a brain aneurysm and had died in his sleep. Ever since then, it seems like every headache I have makes me worried that I could be having an aneurysm too.

A few weeks after he died, a flower delivery arrived at their house with a dozen red roses for Evon on Valentine's Day. When she called to thank the flower shop, she found out he had ordered them the day before he passed.

The family was growing up. Kevin married his high school sweetheart, Katrina. They had a big wedding at Epworth, and Gerry did the service. A few years later, they had a daughter, Alexis, my first great-grandbaby, followed by Taylor a few years later. After a long courtship, Tim married Donna, and they have a daughter, Jaila. It was a packed house to have the whole family over for our pre-Christmas dinners. It would have made Gerard so happy to see everyone together.

Howard and Kathleen divorced in the early 1980s, and he lived a bachelor life ever since. He started having trouble with his back in the 1990s. It started after a fall that he had at work. It would get better, and then he would move the wrong way, and it would cause trouble again.

Howard had mostly worked in grocery stores with produce. He always knew how to pick out the best fruit. He would tell me if you knock on a melon just so you can tell if it's sweet or not. It worked for him but not for me. It seemed like whatever I picked out was too hard or too soft and never tasted as good as what he brought home.

Eventually, he was having so much trouble with his back that he was off work more than he was on. And eventually, he lost his job altogether. There wasn't much other work he could do, not at his age; everything he knew how to do was manual, and his body wouldn't allow that. He asked to move back home so he could save to get back on his feet. Of course, I welcomed him back with open arms.

A woman from our church, Jackie, had recently divorced from her husband. Every now and then, she would join the lunch bunch with Esther and Rita. I think it lifted her spirits. She loved to crochet like me, so she would come by the house, and we would crochet together and try new patterns. She was an only child, and her parents were both deceased, so she didn't have much family. We adopted her into ours.

Since she was coming by the house more, she and Howard met and started talking. I think they could commiserate with each other. They were both at a place in their life where they never thought they'd be. Howard, injured and living at home with his mother in his mid-fifties, and Jackie, newly single with two children in her late forties. They started being together more and more, going out and doing more things. Both of their spirits were lifting. Howard and Jackie decided to marry in June of 1999. They had a small ceremony in the chapel at Epworth, Gerry's church, and he did the service. It was such a beautiful day.

Reflections on Moving Forward

The 1990s offered many transitions for our family. It was a time of births, deaths, marriages, graduations, and new beginnings. The decade opened with Grandpa's death, but it brought with it so many opportunities to celebrate.

For me, these were my awkward teenage years where I was discovering who I was and what I wanted to be. As for most teenagers, this was a time when I mostly focused on myself. The events of our family were happening around me, and I paid little attention to them. I barely remember the weddings and funerals. I missed Uncle Howard and Aunt Jackie's nuptials and Jason's high school graduation while I was studying abroad in Ghana.

It was breakfast with Grandma that kept me connected and caring at all about what was going on in the family. It was also the time when I was closest to her. Sharing prayers and stories over blueberry muffins is what planted the seed for the development of this book. It is where I learned how she wielded quiet strength, unwavering faith, and a commitment to seeing the success of others.

The Making of a Pearl

I applied to Duke early decision and got my acceptance letter in December, around the time of one of our pre-Christmas celebrations at Grandma's. She asked me about tuition and fees, and I told her about the required $500 commitment fee and how I was frustrated by the inconvenient timing of being due around the holidays. I did not say that to ask for funds or to imply that it was a hardship for us.

However, before leaving for the night, Grandma pressed an envelope into my hand. I opened it on the short car ride home to find five crisp one-hundred dollar bills inside. I started crying and handed it to my parents. My father was upset at the implication that we couldn't afford it. I was embarrassed that somehow I had unintentionally asked for the funds.

Grandma made neither of these assumptions. She prided herself on being able to pay for Dad and Uncle Vernon's college education. I think her intention was to play some small part in that for me, her first grandchild to go to college. Throughout my college years, like she did for Bertie, she would send care packages with notes on updates from home and homemade cookies. I'm okay that she didn't send the Vienna sausages.

During this time period, many things were happening, but nothing was dramatic enough to fully capture my teenage attention. That is how time works; whether you are paying attention or not, life's events keep happening. Not every period is filled with drama. Thank God for that.

Pearls are made slowly, over time. It is in periods of calm that a pearl develops its protective barrier, grows in size, and develops its brilliance.

Chapter 14
Holy Lands, Family Lands

Jason and Gerry baptize Pearl in the Jordan River

Thanksgiving at the Bells

The Making of a Pearl

Above all, maintain constant love for one another, for love covers a multitude of sins.

1 Peter 4:8 (NRS)

In the spring of 1998, I got to go on the trip of a lifetime. Gerry's church was hosting a trip to the Holy Lands with some of the youth. Gerry asked me if I wanted to go, and I said of course. This was not a trip to be missed. There were about ten of us, half youth, half adults. Of course, my traveling partner, Bertie, came too.

We visited Bethlehem, Jerusalem, and so many of the holy sites. One of the most memorable sites was when we visited Petra. Moses passed through here when leading the Israelites out of Egypt. He struck a rock that then poured out water so the people and their livestock could drink. It was a long walk in, and I didn't think I could do it, but I didn't want to miss anything. So, Bertie and I rode in on horseback. Oh my, I hadn't been on a horse since I was a girl. What a bumpy ride; I was hanging on for dear life. The city was just so beautiful, and it was amazing to see how they had carved all of the buildings out of stone.

The bathrooms throughout the trip left a lot to be desired. One time we were on the bus, and one of the girls just had to go. She couldn't wait for the next rest area, so the driver pulled over. Next thing you know, she's out in the bushes making water. When we did finally get to a toilet, it was just an outhouse with a hole in the ground. That was another thing that brought me back to my youth. At least when I was growing up, the outhouse had something to sit on.

The highlight of the trip was being baptized in the Jordan River, the same river where Jesus was baptized so long ago. We all changed into white robes and walked down to the water's edge. Gerry and Jason took each of us in one by one and leaned us back under the water. With each of us, Gerry said, "Remember your baptism." It was such a special moment to be in such a holy place with my son and grandson.

The teens that went on that trip with us are all now grown, and most of them are married with children of their own. Gerry brought water back from the Jordan River and has used that to baptize each of his grandsons. A couple years later, the church sponsored a mission trip to Zimbabwe to visit an orphanage and Africa University. Gerry went along with Rita, Kisha, Maya, and several others from the church. When I was younger, I wanted to be a missionary, but I was too old for missionary work now. I let that trip go on without me.

When I was growing up, land was very important. My father took great pride in giving me and each of my siblings a plot of land. Each of us owned about an acre, and we collectively owned the homeplace where we grew up. Gerard bought land in the same area; he used one acre for a small farm and gave an acre each to Gerry and Vernon. Gerry and Esther had both built houses on their plots, but no one else did. Howard had planned to build at the same time Gerry did, but that never happened.

Despite living elsewhere, my siblings were each continuing to pay ever-increasing property taxes on their land. They were each getting older and not richer. Upton died, and we took over his payments. Melvin had also passed, and his sons David and Dwight were taking over his payments. In the late 1990s, housing developers started looking to buy the land that Papa had given me and my siblings, and my siblings were very interested in selling.

I did not want them to sell, and neither did Gerry or Vernon. So much was being built up all around that very little land remained, especially land owned by Blacks. But our friends and neighbors were selling their family farms and getting lots of money for them.

We sold the homeplace where we grew up, and the developer turned it into a cul de sac with six big houses. We talked about it for a long time, but once a developer approached us, it went fast. Eugene was living there at the time, and he quickly found a new place to live. He didn't have much to clean out, and a lot of what there wasn't worth saving. I couldn't watch as they tore the house down. At least we got them to name the street Hallman Court, to have some connection to the past.

The land my siblings and I owned was bigger than the homeplace, eight acres in all. My piece was the first and the entryway to the rest of it. They needed me to sell for them to be able to sell theirs, and that I did not want to do. So, they sued me. My brothers and sisters, who I had helped raise, got through high school, and sent off to war, were suing me over land.

The family dynamics started to change. We didn't spend the holidays all together like we used to. We used to spend Thanksgiving with Melvin and Evon. After he died, we'd all go to Jackie and Howard's. But when all of the land stuff started, it seemed less enjoyable to all be together like that. Rita started hosting

The Making of a Pearl

Thanksgiving, and Vernon and I would go there. Esther would host the rest of the family.

I got a lawyer, Mr. Brown, he was a good lawyer, and he knew land and property. We had worked with him for years when Gerard would buy land for houses. He was one of the few White lawyers who would work with Blacks back then. The suit over family land went back and forth. He stalled things for years, but eventually, he got them to buy me out.

While my siblings had been talking about selling their land for years, they hadn't had any success. Then, finally, they had one interested developer. Esther and Curtis and the Talleys moved out. Their houses were torn down. Gerry and Vernon never sold their plots. Gerry's house still stands, and the new neighborhood went up around it. They replaced those two houses with thirty single-family and townhomes. They named one of the streets Samuel Manor Court after my father, and at the entrance to the development is a marker recognizing the Hallman family.

Initially, Esther and Curtis had planned to move back to the development, but the houses were big, and they got comfortable living in a smaller space without all the upkeep. They all got money. I don't know how much exactly, but I'm sure it was a significant amount. Thompkins bought a brand-new car for the first time in over twenty years. Here's the funny thing, he bought the exact same car he had before, just a newer version. Esther, Thompkins, and Bertie all went on a cruise to the Panama Canal. Thompkins was always tight with his money and had never cruised before, so I guess he got enough to feel comfortable splurging a little.

Amazingly, through all of this, Esther, Rita, and I continued our Wednesday lunches. There were always plenty of other things to talk about besides the land. We let our lawyers do the fighting over that. There is nothing more important than family, and just because you are having a disagreement over one thing doesn't mean you can't talk and have a good time about something else. It doesn't hurt them if I hold a grudge; it only hurts me, so what is the use of carrying pain around in your heart? It doesn't mean I wasn't upset about what was happening, but I didn't let it destroy me or our relationship.

In the fall of 2003, I hadn't been feeling well for a few days, and one day I woke up early in the morning with a bad stomachache. I went to the bathroom, and my bowel movement was black and sticky and mixed with blood. That scared me, so after I got myself cleaned up, I called Vernon to come take me to the hospital. They ran a bunch of tests and found that I had colon cancer.

They scheduled surgery for the next day; the family was there to pray over me before I went in. Esther and I always have a deal that we are the last ones to see each other before we go into surgery and the first ones to see each other when we get out. We always take each other's teeth so that they don't get lost and that no one else sees us without our teeth in. Even in my eighties, I still had a little vanity.

I went through the surgery just fine. They told me they had cut out a section of my colon, and luckily they didn't find any more cancer, so I didn't need chemotherapy or any more treatment. I don't think I would have wanted it even if they told me I needed it. You have to die of something. Oddly the thing that was keeping me in the hospital was that I needed to move my bowels. The nurses were cheering for me when I passed gas, and it was a big celebration when I finally had a bowel movement. Even though they told me that I was cancer free, I still live with the fear that it will come back.

Reflections on Holy Lands, Family Lands

The land in Grandma's family was another kind of holy land. Her father had purchased it and doled out an acre to each of his children. I know both my grandfather and my grandmother's father were proud of the land they acquired and even more proud to give it away. I even snagged a piece of it, building a house on what used to be my grandfather's small one-acre farm.

What is more remarkable than their owning land is that my grandmother and her sister, Aunt Esther, managed to continue their weekly lunch bunch throughout the land feud. Every now and then, when I was home would join them for lunch. You would never have known anything was going on in the background. I think Grandma was hurt that her siblings sued her over the land, but in the end, they got what they needed, and she did what she needed to preserve the relationship.

Unlike Grandpa, who relished scaring children by popping out his teeth and giving a gummy grin, Grandma never took her teeth out. I never saw teeth soaking in cleaner or tubes of denture adhesive in the bathroom. I've shared a room with her, and she never takes her teeth out. Part of me knew that she had to have false teeth; they were just too perfect to be hers. But it wasn't until I caught a glimpse of the denture exchange with Aunt Esther that I had confirmation that her teeth were not attached.

As the Avon lady, Grandma prides herself on looking her best. She wouldn't dare go to the hospital without makeup, jewelry, and her hair done or a hat to cover if it wasn't. One time when she called the paramedics, she looked so good that they didn't believe she was the one that needed to go to the hospital. She was the walking advertisement for the products she peddled. She also knew that, as a Black woman, looks mattered. She always sought to present herself to medical personnel with a look that said, "I'm here. I'm worthy; listen to me!

I was in medical school when Grandma was diagnosed with colon cancer. It happened to fall when we had a break, and I was able to come down and spend a few days there while she was in the hospital. She, as always, was resilient. I wasn't there when they had conversations with the doctor about her treatment plan. I don't know if she wasn't offered advanced treatment because they truly did not find more cancer or because they believed someone in their late eighties wouldn't live long enough to benefit. But either way, she is a fifteen-plus-year cancer survivor, and despite her worry that it will return, praise God, it hasn't.

As a medical student, visiting family in the hospital brought challenges and conflicting emotions. I could see the pride in my family. Grandma introduced me to every medical person that walked in the room, "That's my granddaughter. She's going to be a doctor."

When you are the doctor in the family, people look to you to know the answers. Then and now, I am always willing to help them the best I can. I became a family physician not just because I love caring for patients and their families but because I don't mind answering my own family's questions. From being inside the medical field, I know just how difficult it is for the layperson to navigate the medical system. I always strive to be a translator of medical jargon and to explain the complex process that is our healthcare system.

Chapter 15
Pain and Presidents

Pain and Presidents

The Greens visit President Barack Obama in the Oval Office

The Making of a Pearl

> *³Praise be to the God and Father of our Lord Jesus Christ, the Father of compassion and the God of all comfort, ⁴who comforts us in all our troubles, so that we can comfort those in any trouble with the comfort we ourselves receive from God.*
>
> *2 Corinthians 1:3-4 (NIV)*

Jason started working on the presidential campaign of Barack Obama while he was in law school. It never seemed possible that a Black man could be president. It seemed like a jinx to even say it out loud. I prayed for his safety constantly. We were amazed when he won. Jason went to work for him in the White House. I could hardly believe it; one of my grandchildren was working at the White House with President Obama, the first Black president.

Jason worked in the White House for five years, and when he was finished, he got to bring the family into the White House to take a picture with the President. What a day that was. They brought my wheelchair because it was going to be a long way to walk from the street to the White House. I didn't have any intention of sitting in it for the picture. When we got to the White House, we had to wait for a while in the lobby.

They called us back to the parlor right outside President Obama's office, and we waited a bit more. Then they opened the door to yet another room before entering the Oval Office, where President Obama would be waiting for us. To our surprise, he was waiting for us in that little room. He bent down and gave me a hug and kiss on the cheek. They started to roll me into the oval office, and I said, "No, no, I can't have a wheelchair in my picture with the president."

President Obama leaned over and said, "Of course you can, Mrs. Green; you are just as beautiful." And he rolled me into the Oval Office himself. Well, that was that. He was so gracious.

The room was smaller than I expected it to be, but as soon as you went in, you could feel the weight of it. It was almost magical. He chatted with us a bit and didn't seem rushed. He gave big hugs to Kisha's boys. We took the photo, and then our family went out to dinner. What an amazing day. Who would have thought that a poor girl like me from little Quince Orchard would get to meet the President of the United States? And having lived through segregation and all of the injustices of Black people, who would have thought that our President would be Black?

I was starting to feel my age. I was still selling Avon and volunteering at Asbury, but around age ninety-two, I started having trouble with my vision. My vision got so bad that I didn't trust myself driving anymore. This was really hard for me. I was used to always being on the go and going wherever I needed to whenever I wanted to. But I didn't let not driving stop me.

Esther would drive me to Asbury so I could volunteer, and others would take me out when I needed to go somewhere. I wasn't used to having to depend on others to do things for me; I was always the one who would do it for someone else. I hated to inconvenience people by asking them to do something small for me, like getting yarn for a new crochet pattern. But everyone was happy to help me, and I felt the love coming back to me that I had put out.

In 2013, the locusts started circling. By locusts, I mean my foot started acting up again. Every fifteen to twenty years, just like locusts, it seems to start to cause trouble again. It started with pain in my heel and traveled up my whole leg to my hip. It was so bad I would just cry out at night. My doctor's office had closed, so now I started going to Kisha's office at a new practice she started in Gaithersburg.

They brought me in and tried all kinds of new things for the pain, like acupuncture. I never did get used to those needles. Ultimately, I went to the hospital. My foot had an infection in it that had gone to the bone. The doctors were talking about surgery and that they would need to cut off my foot because the circulation was poor and the wound wouldn't heal.

I was in the hospital for a while, and then I started rehabilitation, and guess where they sent me—Asbury! Oh, there were so many familiar faces there. I knew most of the nurses and some of the residents. I hadn't been able to go as often as before, but I still knew many people. The nurses took such good care of me, and there was always someone stopping by to say hello. And, of course, I had to have an Avon book for them to look at.

Here it was, almost ninety years from when I first started having trouble with my foot, and they were telling me the same thing that they told me back then. That they would have to cut it off. Back then, I had an angel of mercy who helped me save my foot. This time, I had another, in my granddaughter, Kisha, a doctor.

I set my mind that they would not take my foot, and I would walk again. I prayed over it constantly. And did my exercises and took my medicines. And I did save my foot and walk again. Eventually, I was able to go back home and was able to walk okay. I had a cane, but I usually kept it folded up in my purse and used it only in case of emergencies. So long ago, that nurse taught me to take care of my foot myself, and to this day, I continue to do that. I bathe it and soak it, watch and pray over it.

As my foot was getting better, my hip was getting worse. I hadn't had pain in my side like this before, and it just kept progressing. It didn't seem possible that so much pain was coming from this one joint. I worried that it was my colon cancer coming back or some other problem that they couldn't find. But the doctors just kept saying it was only my hip.

I started physical therapy and started taking strong medication for pain. I had been able to walk but wasn't doing that as well. At first, I would just carry my cane with me in my purse, but then I had to actually start using it. Then I started using the walker and then the wheelchair. For a while, after my foot got better, I could walk up to the communion rail at church, but eventually, I couldn't do that anymore either.

One night it got so bad that I pressed my LifeAlert button to go to the hospital. I didn't tell Vernon first because he would have told me not to go, but I figured I paid my insurance; it was my right to go. By the time the paramedics got there, I was dressed with my makeup on and sitting in my wheelchair, ready to go. Well, when I got to the hospital, things just went from bad to worse.

They said they were going to do the MRI that my doctor was trying to get, but they never did. They changed my pain medication. I didn't know I could be in worse pain than what I was already in, but they sure did find a way. I ended up spending Mother's Day in the hospital, probably the worst Mother's Day I'd ever had. I was one hundred years old, and it made me wonder if I even wanted to make it to see one hundred and one, being in all this pain.

They finally let me go, and Kisha arranged for me to get a steroid shot in my hip. That helped more than what they had done for me in the hospital. I learned that they can't really help me there. And what I've come to accept is that this pain is not going to leave me. I have it every day. Some days are better than others. Nights are just awful. Growing old is not for the weak. My legs are now too weak to walk, so I'm in the wheelchair all day. I do try to get to church, at least for communion, but sometimes it is just too painful transferring from the wheelchair to the car and back. My bladder won't hold, and the pain medicines make me constipated. But that doesn't mean I'm giving up.

Many days I wonder why I'm still here, but if I wake up, then that means God has something for me to do that day. I haven't been to Asbury since I was a patient there myself, but I do still sell a little Avon. Rita helps me with the orders. It isn't much now, just my loyal few, but it gives me something to do. And every day, I try to call someone to check on them and give them some encouragement. And that encourages me too.

In the middle of all this pain, I turned one hundred years old. I never thought I would see the day. My parents never lived this long, though several in our community did. Big Howard's father lived to one hundred and four, and Big Howard's sister was over one hundred as well. We had my birthday party at a large reception hall at Asbury; how fitting for it to be there. It was so nice to have all the family and friends together.

We had a big celebration, even bigger than the surprise party they had for me when I turned seventy. Even some of Rita's family from Ohio came to help celebrate. Kisha's boys read Psalm 23, and Vernon sang a song he wrote just for me. The county declared June 18th as Ida Pearl Green Day. I wasn't going to miss that day; just the excitement of coming together helped push me forward.

There was so much to celebrate that year. It was also the one-hundred-fiftieth anniversary of when they purchased the land for the schoolhouse and Pleasant View church. We had a big celebration for that the weekend after my birthday. It was our eightieth family reunion. We had it at a hotel this year, a step up from when we started in Mama and Papa's backyard. And it was the fiftieth anniversary of Fairhaven's creation, another celebration. I was so happy to live to see all of it. Having something to look forward to always makes me happy.

Reflections on Pain and Presidents

I went to visit Grandma on her actual one-hundredth birthday, which was a few days after the big celebration. She was doing her laundry. I laughed and said, "Well, I guess if you are still doing laundry at one hundred, I will never escape it."

What Grandma never lost as she aged was a sense of purpose and a goal to be of service. The only thing she ever said she was too old to do was wear blue jeans. Her philosophy was that she would

The Making of a Pearl

keep doing it until she couldn't, and then she'll find someone else to do it.

Jason and I both had the honor of working for the Obama administration. He, as White House Council, and I as a White House Fellow. Jason started on the Obama campaign while he was in law school at Yale and then joined the administration just after graduation. As a fellow, I spent a year at the US Department of Agriculture working on food safety net programs. We both had an amazing experience.

In a way, it was also like coming full circle in our family. Grandma started her career in government service, yet the difference in our experiences is striking. She endured discrimination, being turned away from jobs and passed over for promotions. She put up with the horrible conditions in a dank and dirty VA basement where she sorted war records.

Those experiences contrast greatly with the experiences Jason and I have, like celebrating our mom's birthday at the White House bowling alley, watching fireworks from the White House lawn, and toasting with eggnog at the White House Christmas Party. The stark difference is truly amazing.

I often reflect on the investments made by our ancestors so many years ago in this Quince Orchard community that made it possible for me and my siblings to get where we are. Post-slavery, newly freed Gary and Matilda Green could have gone anywhere. The fact that they settled and remained here, in Quince Orchard, just outside of Washington, DC, would end up being pivotal in my career trajectory. Even more so, the following generations continued to set up shop right here. My grandmother lived less than a mile from her parents. My parents are half a mile from her. Just an acre of land separates me from my parents. With how we are going, my children will never leave home.

My grandmother's parents helped her raise Howard, and she helped Jason, Maya, and me, and my parents continue the tradition with my three boys. When I did the fellowship, I was married with two young kids. I would not have even considered the fellowship if Washington, DC, was not within commuting distance. While several men in my fellowship class picked up and moved their families to DC to participate in the fellowship, that would not have worked for mine. Nor could I have done it without the support of my parents close by. Women can't have it all; no one can. But you can get closer *when you live close to work and have a strong family support network.*

After the fellowship, I helped to start a primary care practice in Gaithersburg. It envisioned practicing medicine as it always should be, holistically with the patient at the center. Our four pillars of wellness: eat well, move more, stress less, and connect deeply, are lessons to live life by. And when I think of my grandmother, she abided by these for most of her life.

Grandma's age was finally catching up with her once she reached her nineties. Her declining eyesight, followed by problems with her foot and hip, led to a shrinking of her world. Grandpa used to call her the Road Runner because she was always going somewhere or doing something. And this period of having to sit and be waited on was and still is difficult for her.

Grandma was always an active person and started her day with exercises. I remember one Christmas when she was in her eighties, and she pulled out an ab roller. No one believed she could really do it, so she got down on the floor and showed us that she could. Today, being confined mostly to a wheelchair makes leaving the house difficult. Subsequently, her ability to move, exercise, and be active is waning.

Grandma shared with Jason, who then relayed to me that she was equating me to that nurse—the angel of mercy, as she calls her—who saved her foot as a child. I don't have healing powers, but I do know how to gather a team and bring the best resources together. Pain is a cruel beast, and it is hard to watch someone, especially a loved one, in pain. We tried everything from acupuncture to narcotics. I even tried, unsuccessfully, to get her a medical marijuana card. Ultimately, time, prayer, and good ol' grin and bear it is what gets her through each day.

The COVID-19 pandemic was especially challenging. Before that, while it was difficult for her to get out, people could come to her, and a daily stream of visitors would come by. The Wednesday lunch dates with Aunt Esther still continued; she just brought food to Grandma instead of them going out. With COVID-19, all of that had to go on pause. No one wanted to be the one who gave Grandma COVID-19. Her ability to connect deeply was being diminished.

We are blessed that Uncle Vernon, who moved in with her and Grandpa when he grew ill, continues to live with her today. His care and nursing have allowed her to remain at home past the century

The Making of a Pearl

mark. And while his tolerance for visitors is much lower than hers, his nurturing is also what helps to keep her going.

In April 2023, the US Surgeon General issued an advisory raising alarm for an epidemic of loneliness. The report stresses the importance of social connections as a healing and protective factor for individual and population health, resilience, and prosperity. For Grandma, when she has a social event or something to look forward to, she, like many of us, can put her pain aside.

Even when she was in pain, she would say things like, "Well, Maya is graduating in a few months or so and so's wedding is coming up. So, I have to keep living for that." When COVID-19 paused the world, when there was nothing to look forward to—no outings or parties, or even visitors to greet—that was not just hard, it was physically painful.

She reached her one-hundred-second birthday in the midst of the COVID-19 worldwide pandemic. Ironically she was born in 1918, amidst the Spanish Flu pandemic to which COVID-19 is often compared. Grandma will turn one-hundred-five on June 18, 2023. If you ask her how she is doing, she will say she feels like she is one-hundred-five. She has survived two worldwide pandemics, a life-threatening foot infection, debilitating hip arthritis, diminished hearing and eyesight, colon cancer, and most recently, breast cancer.

Yet she is blessed with an excellent memory. She has lived through the death of her parents, four brothers, two husbands, and a host of friends and family. Her faith has only deepened through tragedy, and she continues to be thankful for the riches she has received. Some days are hard, painful days, and others are cheery. And we are all thankful to have had so much time with her and treasure every additional moment.

> [45] Again, the kingdom of heaven is like a merchant looking for fine pearls. [46] When he found one of great value, he went away and sold everything he had and bought it.
>
> Matthew 13:45-46 (NIV)

Epilogue

Kisha and Grandma Pearl

[4]Love is patient, love is kind. It does not envy, it does not boast, it is not proud. [5]It is not rude, it is not self-seeking, it is not easily angered, it keeps no record of wrongs. [6]Love does not delight in evil but rejoices with the truth. [7]It always protects, always trusts, always hopes, always perseveres... [13]And now these three remain: faith, hope and love. But the greatest of these is love.

I Corinthians 13:4-7, 13 (NIV)

Grandma Pearls

- Love everyone. Forgive everyone.
- It's not worth fighting over. If you are right, eventually, people will see that. And if you aren't right but don't know it yet, it's better that you stop arguing and save yourself the embarrassment.
- Be considerate of other people.
- Love God and read your bible.
- Find a way to help someone.
- Don't hold a grudge.
- When hard times come, God is there.
- You can always be of service to others.

About the Author

Dr. Kisha Davis, Pearl's granddaughter, is a compassionate family physician and public health leader. She is wife to educator Everett Davis and mother to three amazing sons. She and her brother, Jason Green, co-produced *Finding Fellowship*, a documentary about the history of the Quince Orchard Community. Together with her sister, Dr. Maya Green, she co-hosted the podcast, *The Sisters Will See You Now*.

Kisha learned her grandmother's stories over the breakfast table in high school. Pearl's life story and the lessons learned from it are too precious to lose. The desire to honor her legacy compelled Kisha to write this biography, capturing the essence of a woman whose impact will be felt for generations to come.

www.ingramcontent.com/pod-product-compliance
Lightning Source LLC
Chambersburg PA
CBHW031320160426
43196CB00007B/602